A **WESTERN HORSEMAN** BOOK

WORLD CLASS REINING

Proven Techniques and Winning Show Ring Strategies

By
Shawn Flarida & Craig Schmersal
With Kathy Swan

Edited by Cathy Martindale
Photography by John Brasseaux
Diagrams by Ron Bonge

World Class Reining

Published by
WESTERN HORSEMAN® **magazine**

3850 North Nevada Ave.
Box 7980
Colorado Springs, CO 80933-7980

www.westernhorseman.com

Design, Typography, and Production
Western Horseman
Fort Worth, Texas

Front & Back Cover Photos By
John Brasseaux

Printing
Branch Smith
Fort Worth, Texas

Manufactured in the United States of America

First Printing: April 2007

ISBN 978-0-911647-78-3

CONTENTS

DEDICATION

I dedicate this book to my three greatest gifts, my children — Cody, Courtney, and Sam. You make me a better horse trainer and, more importantly, a better person. I love you.

ACKNOWLEDGEMENTS

My clients: My life and career have been influenced by many great people to whom I owe a great deal of thanks. A special thanks to the people who believed in my talent from the beginning of my career. You all stuck by me when I struggled to make the old brown and tan Chevy payments.

Randy Bartley (my very first client), Harold Brewer, Kim and Allen Crupper, my brother and friend Mark Flarida, Mike Harper, Carol Harris, Brian Hoffman, Jeff and Cheree Kirkbride, John Mehaffey, Danny Roe, Mark Schols, Rosanne Sternberg Bob Stinner and so many others.

The horses: Certain horses have shaped my life and made my achievements possible.

Tinny Tiny — You taught me all about "barn-balkiness."

Morse Generator — You gave your heart and forever touched mine.

Dun Its Easter Bunny — My first All American Quarter Horse Congress victory.

Major Incident — You taught the world that it's okay to enjoy your life's work. What a fun ride for a young cowboy.

Freckles Top Prize — A little horse with a big heart. You will always be one of my favorites.

San Jo Freckles — You never let me down, even when the odds were against us.

Wimpys Little Step — You gave me the greatest gift of my career — confidence.

Smart Spook — The second time was even sweeter than the first.

KR Lil Conquistador — A surprise to everyone but us and one of my greatest horse friends.

My best friend: Sam Ely — You make me laugh even when I shouldn't.

To Matthew Parson: Please know that I am so proud of the man you are and grateful for the chance to be a part of your life. You are one of the greatest people I know.

My family: You have and will be the most important part of my life. Mom and Dad (Bill and Betty Flarida) taught me love, respect, work ethic and so much more. Michele, my wife, teaches me every day that love is endless, and our children (Cody, Courtney, and Sam) remind me daily that love is unconditional. The greatest part of my job is that I get to be the man they cheer for. I thank God for every day I get to be so blessed.

To my fans in heaven: My brother Clint Flarida and my friend and mother-in-law Becky Hanby, you ride with me every step and we miss you.

Shawn Flarida

DEDICATION

To my wife, Ginger – Thank you for being my best friend, biggest fan and best critic. You're honest and don't always tell me what I want to hear, but I respect you for that. Thank you for believing in me when all I had was $200 and a few saddles and bridles to my name. Thanks for driving and staying awake with me all night at horse shows. Also, for having the vision and courage to invest our money in the horses I love. And, mostly for giving me a family and always believing in me. I love you.

ACKNOWLEDGEMENTS

Dad (Chuck Schmersal): For sacrificing and dedicating yourself completely to make sure my dream of becoming a horse trainer came true.

Mike and Linda Flarida: For taking me, an 8-year-old boy, and his 2-year-old horse in training.

Bill, Betty and Shawn Flarida: For putting up with me all those summers and feeding me chocolate cake and iced tea.

My New York extended family: Joe Annunziata, Priscilla Honkana, Tony Lomangino, Sue Lomangino, Annie Mucaria, Charlie and Stephanie Rome, Dave Tina and Henry, Elaine and Vinnie Uvino: For taking a chance on me when I was 17 and making me feel like a part of your family.

The trainers: Bob Anthony, Don Boyd, Dutch Chapman, Bob Loomis, Tim McQuay and Randy Paul — Who took a special interest in me.

My clients: Who believed in me and continue to support my dream.

My sons: Chris and Nick, for keeping me young and giving me an excuse to play, I love you.

My in-laws: David and Lyn Bishop: For the support you gave your daughter when she married a cowboy. And for always taking my side.

The horses:
  Set The Pace — My first bronze trophy winner.

  Cee Blair Sailor: My first world champion.

Side Smoke — The biggest heart I ever rode.

Mister Diamond Dun It — My first open NRHA Futurity finalist.

Tidal Wave Jack — The biggest stopping horse I've ever ridden. You exceeded my dreams of what we could accomplish together.

Mister Montana Nic — I can always count on you.

Commanders Nic — The pony we bought for the kids that won $256,000. You made riding and training fun every day and seem easy. You were always a threat to the competition and gave me the confidence to know I had a chance to win every time I walked through the gate. Sorry, kids, for stealing your pony.

Wrangle Whiz — The little horse with a lot of talent.

Mr Dual Rey — Another one I can count on. Thank you, Holly Casey.

My closest friends: Mike McEntire, Tyson Randle: You never make horse shows seem like work.

And finally, my family: Who continue to give their support and are always there for me.

FOREWORD

The past 30 years have been a whirlwind time of change and growth for the reining world. The industry has changed from an era when we rode lots of horses and a few reiners to a time of specialization.

A highly athletic and specialized horse has evolved – one that has been bred and raised to do the maneuvers in a superb manner. The reining horses we are privileged to ride today are from families of equines who have been distinguished in the reining arena. Not just one or two generations, but multiple sires and grandsires can claim prominence.

Riders, as well, have honed their skills and training techniques — each generation learning from those from a mere decade before.

Craig and Shawn have been extremely successful and are a very visible and instrumental part of reining's present and will be part of its future. I congratulate them for their role in continuing to grow and promote our industry.

Tim McQuay

PREFACE

For both Craig and Shawn, the sport of reining is much more than a career; it's a way of life. As with many who are involved with reining, they pour their hearts into achieving the perfect pattern. They've been rewarded for their dedicated efforts with tremendous success, but most of all they treasure the respect and friendships they've developed with their horses and other reiners.

In this sport, the respect between rider and horse is unparalleled. Reiners are truly blessed to ride some of the most physically talented equine athletes known to man. The incredible runs that define our sport have been achieved when trust and mutual respect are the foundation of the horse/human relationship. This kind of dedication is demonstrated every day in and out of the arena, and, as a spectator, I'm always amazed how two so completely different beings can meld into one fabulous display of athleticism. These horses trust us with their lives, and we trust them with our hopes and dreams. The result is a partnership that endures beyond the arena.

The same goes for the relationships between riders. Respect for one another forges great friendships that make their achievements unforgettable and their failures forgivable. People associated with reining are always very willing to lend a helping hand to other riders, whether in the arena or at home in times of crisis. This camaraderie is one of the sport's greatest attributes. Although reiners are highly competitive, good sportsmanship is hallmark and ever-present. Now that reining has become an international sport, friendships span oceans. The universality of the word "whoa" unites people who otherwise would never have met. We travel, work and ride together as one big family. Diverse people, backgrounds and ideas blend to make a great sport even better. Through participation, new friendships are born every day.

For Craig and Shawn, the ability to be successful in their careers with their families and friends as their cheering sections is a great gift. For us, to be able to watch the people we love achieve their dreams is an even greater gift.

Michele Flarida

INTRODUCTION

Welcome to the exciting world of reining! We're passionate about our sport, and we think you'll find out why in the pages of this book. In it, we hope to take you on a journey, so come along with us for the ride of your life.

We start by offering you our best advice on selecting a reining horse and maintaining him in peak performance condition. From there we explain our approach to training and how to provide your horse with a solid foundation in the basics, so he's prepared for the highly technical maneuvers a reining horse must perform. The maneuvers themselves are introduced in a logical, step-by-step fashion — one builds upon the other in a beautiful dance called reining. Lastly, we include proven show-pen strategies that have worked well for us, and they will for you, too.

Don't let the fancy maneuvers you see in reining competition intimidate you. You can and will be able to master them with a little help from this book, probably a mentor or two and, of course, lots of hard work and dedication on your part.

You can certainly train your own horse; however, it'd be best if you sought the help of a professional reining horse trainer as your mentor and advisor. Developing a relationship with a pro is a wise thing to do. He or she should be someone who can answer your questions if you get in a jam. Both of us are pros, yet we still consult with one another all the time, especially when we meet at horse shows. So, as long as you get competent help and some direction, training your own horse isn't a bad idea at all.

If, however, you have a 2-year-old (or whatever age) horse who's really tough-minded, don't attempt to train him yourself. Give him to a professional who knows how to handle such horses. Riding a rank horse is dangerous, and we're not here to explain how to do that in this book. Actually, we advise against trying to work with that type of horse. For the purposes of this book, we assume that you have a quiet, well-behaved horse, one that accepts training well. Otherwise, you'll have great difficulty training something as technical as a reining horse. Reaction times on horses are so quick. We've had friends who've had their necks broken riding unruly horses. So before you begin your journey, we strongly recommend making sure you have a good, trainable animal to work with.

Our best advice is to first buy an older, experienced reining horse who will teach you as you go. Once you're familiar with the sport and what the maneuvers should feel and look like, you'll be better equipped to attempt training your own horse.

Again, don't be afraid to pick up the phone and ask a pro or, better yet, haul your horse to his barn and train with him once a week so he can check your progress. Having another set of eyes watch you will save you from making big mistakes from which you might not be able to recover. Professionals in the reining horse industry are very willing to help anyone.

That's the main reason why we wanted to write this book. Reining is a great sport and a lot of fun. Good luck on your journey!

"At the heart of this global phenomenon is the reining horse itself."

1

REINING — A GREAT AND GROWING SPORT

Welcome to the fastest growing equine sport in the world — reining! From humble beginnings as just one of many classes offered within the American Quarter Horse Association show system, to the formation of the fledgling National Reining Horse Association in the mid-1960s, to worldwide popularity and acclaim four decades later, the sport has grown exponentially to exceed even its founders' dreams. With its membership doubled in the last decade, the NRHA now has about 90 affiliate organizations in 30 countries, putting on more than 500 sanctioned shows, paying out millions in prize money.

At the heart of this global phenomenon is the reining horse itself — a beautiful, athletic, highly trainable equine. Isn't that what every horse person wants? Whether your goal is to prove your skills and those of your horse in a competitive environment or just ride the prettiest, most broke horse in your neighborhood, the reining horse fills the bill like no other. It's no wonder riders are flocking to the sport by the thousands and breeders are anxiously awaiting the next foal crop after they've crossed one gorgeous athlete with another. The sport is just plain fun, and the awesome reining horse is the main attraction.

Perfection of the Basics

Reining challenges the rider to achieve the highest levels of horsemanship, all of which requires commitment and the cooperation of a superior equine partner. Therein lies reining's appeal. We all strive to be the best horsemen and horsewomen we can be, and we naturally want to ride the best horses possible. Reining gives us both.

Within the sport, you study the nature of the horse, the way the horse moves, its gaits and athletic abilities. Along the way, you'll likely discover your own talents for training and competition. You'll find out who you are when the chips are down and it's your turn to play.

Much like its English cousin dressage, reining is the perfection of horsemanship basics, but in the western disciplines. Being performed at speed, however, elevates the degree of difficulty whether your horse is circling, turning, changing leads, stopping or backing up. Add to the mix the fact that you must be able to guide your horse through a complex pattern with precision and poise, all on a loose rein, and you've got a highly challenging but rewarding experience. The horse isn't the only one learning to handle itself; you become a student as well.

The beautiful, well-broke reining horse is the sport's main attraction.

The United States team for the 2002 World Equestrian Games in Jerez, Spain, won the gold medal and Shawn was the individual gold medalist. Pictured left to right: Craig Johnson, Tom McCutcheon, Scott McCutcheon, Craig Schmersal and Shawn Flarida.

From the Kitchen Table

Reining and the NRHA evolved like most anything else — they sprang to life out of a need. Reining first appeared as an AQHA class in 1950 and for the next decade it progressed from a course that included all three gaits (walk, trot and lope), plus directional changes, to a standardized pattern calling for more complicated maneuvers, such as rollbacks, figure-eights, speed control and stops.

In the mid-1960s, at a large horse show in Chicago, Illinois, the need for a better way to judge reining horses became apparent. Trainer Dale Wilkinson had his assistant trainer Bill Horn ride Continental King for owners Dr. James and Mickie Glenn. (All of the aforementioned people and the horse are now in the NRHA Hall of Fame.) Horn didn't win the class, but Mickie thought he should have and wondered what could be done to improve the judging. Wilkinson suggested that an association be started to standardize the rules.

Shortly thereafter, in 1965, at an AQHA show in Dayton, Ohio, Horn won the reining on Continental King. That sparked a group of reining enthusiasts to come together to promote reining as a single-event sport. Besides Wilkinson, Glenn and Horn, other founders include Stretch and Clark Bradley, Jim Cotton, Paul Horn, R.D. Baker, C.T. Fuller, Bob Anthony and Pat Faitz.

Wilkinson's brainchild came to life in November 1966 when Mickie Glenn (now Mickie Carter) set about to organize a reining horse association literally on her kitchen table. She was the organization's first secretary, and it was through her tireless efforts that the sport survived its early years.

The first NRHA Futurity for 3-year-old reining horses had 35 entries and was held in 1966 in Columbus, Ohio. It was won by Wilkinson riding Pocorochie Bo, owned by Miles Chester. The first-place paycheck for the history-making run $2,400.

WALTENBERRY

Shawn rode Tinsel Nic, owned by Rosanne Sternberg of Sterling Ranch, Aubrey, Texas, to titles at the AQHA World Show in senior reining and the 2006 FEI World Reining Masters (pictured) in Denver, Colorado.

Fast forward 40 years and a lot of growing pains, which include the addition of non-pro, intermediate, limited and youth divisions; the *NRHA Reiner* magazine; NRHA Hall of Fame; NRHA Derby for 4-, 5- and 6-year-olds; an objective judging system; year-end awards; sire and dam program; a move of the corporate office and main events to Oklahoma City; and Million Dollar Horse and Rider designations. Participation and money look a whole lot different, too. Instead of 35 entries, as in the first NRHA Futurity, there are now close to 400 entries, and the winner takes home a guaranteed paycheck for $125,000.

A World View

Beginning in the early to mid-1980s, international interest in reining began to develop. Our top horsemen were constantly flying around the globe, selling horses and giving clinics to an audience thirsty for anything reining. No doubt the strong presence of American Quarter Horses already on the global scene helped jumpstart the sport. Foreigners loved the look and culture of the American "cowboy" and Quarter Horses, and western wear and tack made them feel like John Wayne in the Wild West. It wasn't long before events such as Americana became the biggest equine venues on the European continent. Soon, serious horsemen were paying serious money for America's best blooded reining stock and the sport took off like wildfire.

In the late '80s, the International Reining Council was formed, all with an eye on world-class competition. The goal was to make reining the next Olympic sport, but it would take another decade to be recognized by the Federation Equestre Internationale (FEI), the governing body for international horse sports. Through the dedicated efforts of the NRHA in concert with the AQHA, the dream became a reality. Reining was accepted as the first western discipline on the United States

HAROLD CAMPTON

Harold Campton

Before the NRHA moved its major events to Oklahoma City, and subsequently its corporate headquarters, the association's main events were held at the All American Quarter Horse Congress in Columbus, Ohio. Pictured is Shawn and Lenas Rey Jane winning the open youth reining at the 1987 Congress.

Equestrian Team (now United States Equestrian Federation) in 1998, and the FEI acknowledged it for international competition in 2000. The sport caused quite a stir from the beginning.

Reiners are used to a lot of excitement when they rein. Much hooting, hollering and whistling goes on when a good run is going down. That's in stark contrast to the hushed and quiet audience for dressage, driving or three-day eventing. What a change when the reiners came to town. It wasn't long, though, before the stands at such major events as the World Equestrian Games were filled to capacity with a loud and appreciative crowd of reining enthusiasts. Who doesn't love a good horse race? And reiners can really put on a show at speed.

Reining made its debut at the first WEG in 2002 in Jerez de la Frontera, Spain, and the second took place in Aachen, Germany, in 2006. The World Reining Masters is also a world-class international event that's ushering the sport's march toward the Olympic games.

Your Backyard

Even though the world of reining is getting larger all the time, that doesn't mean you can't enjoy it in your own backyard.

The NRHA international affiliate program has regional clubs that host NRHA-sanctioned shows and other events all over the planet. A group is no doubt close to your home. Join it and become part of a family of like-minded reiners, who compete for fun and prizes but also share a sense of community.

ANDRE BOUGE

ANDRE BOUGE

Top photo: Craig and his stallion Tidal Wave Jack won championships on two continents. They were gold medalists at the 2002 World Equestrian Games in Jerez, Spain, and the 2005 FEI Reining World Masters in Manerbio, Italy (pictured), and winners of the NRBC Derby in Katy, Texas.

Left photo: Eleuterio Arcese, (right), one of Europe's most prominent reining horse breeders and supporters, awards Craig the champion's trophy at the 2005 FEI World Reining Masters. Frank Costantini (left), a former NRHA president and president of the Reining Horse Sports Foundation, was on hand for the presentation.

One of the hallmarks of reining is the camaraderie between exhibitors. Yes, you're all out there to compete against one another, but asking for help is just a smile and a question away. Reiners are famous for their fellowship.

They all know the passion and dedication it takes to rein a horse to NRHA standards, and are more than willing to share their knowledge and experience — pros and amateurs alike. So don't be afraid to ask!

All affiliates offer NRHA-sanctioned shows and their own internal award systems, plus clinics and schooling shows where you can hone your skills. Even if you don't want to compete, an affiliate will introduce you to people who can help you master the sport. If nothing else, your horsemanship and your horse will be better off for it.

The NRHA holds its North American Affiliate Championships at the NRHA

It's your turn to make your dreams come true.

Futurity every year. Reiners who've qualified through the affiliate program come to compete at the same time and on the same hallowed ground at the "big one." What a thrill it is to be riding practically side-by-side with your reining heroes and their amazing horses. There's nothing quite like it.

The Judging System

Probably the single biggest boost to reining's growth has been the sport's judging system, which is touted as the best in the industry. With "think-tank" work provided by veteran reiners Dick Pieper, John Snobelen, Rick Weaver and Dale Wilkinson, the system was instituted in 1985. Until then, NRHA judges evaluated the running of an entire pattern subjectively, and often it seemed that the scores were mostly based on the quality of the horses' stops. But that was then and this is now.

Today's system objectively rates each maneuver on a scale from minus 1½ (extremely poor) to plus 1½ (excellent) with 0 being average. A horse and rider team begins each pattern with a score of 70 and then either zeroes, plusses or minuses the maneu-

vers for a cumulative score. Individual maneuvers include walk-in, stops, spins, rollbacks, circles, back-ups, lead changes, rundowns, run-arounds and hesitation. All NRHA patterns contain every maneuver, divided into groups, some more than once, so a rider and horse are tested thoroughly in the three minutes or so it takes to complete a pattern.

Penalties are assessed for a variety of rule and pattern infractions, such as over- or under-spinning, missing an arena marker, breaking gait, etc. The penalties range from a 0 to minus 5, with a no-score given for serious abuse or misconduct.

A thorough read of the official NRHA Handbook is in order if you plan to compete in any NRHA-sanctioned show. Even local schooling shows and most breed association shows have adopted NRHA's judging standards, so careful attention to the rules and regulations is your responsibility.

The Playing Field

The sport provides as level a playing field as possible, with the NRHA and its affiliates continually looking for new ways to include new people. No matter what your expertise or ambition, the sport has a place for you to begin, grow and achieve.

There are many competition categories. Various classes range from non-professional to pro and literally everything in between. The open and non-pro divisions also include intermediate, limited, limited non-pro, Prime Time (over 50) and novice. Additionally, there are rookie, rookie professional, youth, green-as-grass, snaffle bit, hackamore, freestyle and gelding incentive classes.

Ancillary classes are open to all horses of any breed, aged-events require horses to be of a specific age group, closed aged-events are for the offspring of subscribed stallions and restricted events are for international-level competition. Futurities debut the talents of 3-year-olds and derbies show off 4-, 5- and 6-years olds. The NRHA and its affiliate groups offer both ancillary classes and aged events throughout the year.

As we said, there's something for everyone. The challenge and how high you want to take it are up to you.

The NRHA Handbook describes reining this way: "To rein a horse is not only to guide him, but also to control his every movement. The best reined horse should be willingly guided or controlled with little or no apparent resistance and dictated to completely."

That's a tall order, but it's what reining is all about. In this book we hope to show you just how to do that.

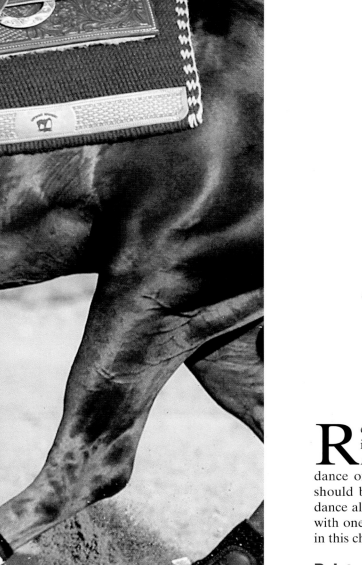

2

SELECTING A REINER

Reining is much like dancing — there are two partners in rhythm with one another, following a dance step. And what's more, there's a leader and a follower. In the dance of reining, obviously you're the leader and your horse should be the willing partner. Whether or not you're able to dance all depends on how well you and your partner are in step with one another. In reining, it all starts with the right horse; so in this chapter, we'll help you pick the right partner.

Pointed in the Right Direction

Finding a reiner can seem overwhelming if you don't know where to start, so getting pointed in the right direction really helps. For that we strongly suggest looking in all the right places,

Beautiful, well-bred, talented, athletic, highly trainable — all are attributes to look for in a reining horse.

and that generally means at the top. Go to major reining horse competitions and watch the riders. Find someone you like – their style, their horses – and introduce yourself. Visit with them, and tell them what you're looking for. They'll be happy to help you in any way they can. Many times they'll have exactly what you need, whether it's a trained, experienced campaigner or a young prospect. Or, at the very least, they can send you in a direction that will benefit you.

You can't go wrong with the top riders because their reputations are very dear to them; they wouldn't want to do anything to damage them. They might tell you where not to go, as well. That, too, reflects on them. They want you to have only good experiences. In this case, word of mouth is their best advertising.

The quickest and best way to find a suitable horse is to seek the help of a professional reining horse trainer.

While the NRHA's major aged-event competitions are great places to find top riders, they might not be conveniently close to your home. If that's the case, go to local and regional events to find someone who might be more within your reach geographically.

Also, in your search, realize that not all trainers have the time to spend with amateur riders. They might not specialize in working with non-professionals. Many do, but not everyone. Some trainers concentrate on the open divisions or aged events only and don't have the time or wherewithal to bring along amateur riders or help them find a horse. They can steer you in the right direction, of course, but it might not be with them if you're just starting out in the industry. So don't feel slighted in the least. It's just that their time is limited mostly to training futurity and derby prospects, leaving little room for anything else. However, they're still the best places to start your research because, for the most part, they've been there and done that and know how to avoid all the pitfalls inherent in learning about the sport and its horses.

That's not to say, though, that top trainers won't have assistants who could help you once you do find a horse. Many A-list trainers employ "good hands" to ride their young stock and these "trainers-in-the-making" might just have time to give lessons. So don't be afraid to ask the "big boys" either; you might be pleasantly surprised.

And, if you do get to hang around a "big barn," then you'll get a firsthand look at how reining is done at the highest level.

The Search is On

Determine your budget ahead of time, whether it's $5,000 or $50,000 and stick to that. It's easy to get lured into paying the big bucks, so stay with your comfort level in the beginning. Just like automobiles, you can upgrade as you go.

Besides trainers, check with well-known breeders for good reining horses and prospects. (Many top trainers are dedicated breeders, as well.) There are literally thousands of top quality breeders in the business. The most serious and reputable ones advertise their breeding programs in the NRHA's *Reiner* magazine; the American Quarter Horse, Paint Horse or Appaloosa Horse Club breed journals or any of the western performance horse-oriented publications, as opposed to local newspapers. Many reliable breeders and trainers have Web sites that allow you to cyber-tour their farms and ranches, get to know them and their breeding and training philosophies and preview their stock for sale.

If you don't live in an area where there are a lot of top reining breeders and trainers, then check online at one of the many reining horse-specific sites. Type "reining" or "reining horse" into a search engine and see what comes up. Also, you can check the classified ad section of equine publications that specialize in western performance horses.

If you buy a horse directly from an individual, whether it's an owner, breeder or trainer, it's always a good idea to have another set of experienced "eyes" come along with you to study the animal. Whether that person is your trainer or a knowledgeable friend, he or she is looking out for your best interests and might see flaws you overlooked. Also, a veterinary pre-purchase exam should be considered a prerequisite for any performance horse or prospect.

Besides purchasing directly from individuals, there's always the horse sale. But beware, there are horse sales and then there are horse sales. Buying a horse at auction can be tricky if you don't know what you're doing. The local sale barn is out; don't even go there unless you enjoy throwing away your money. Your best bet is checking into the sales offered at major aged events, such as the NRHA Futurity and Derby,

and other well-known reining venues. At the very least, these are supported and attended by serious reining horse people who make their living in the industry. The stock should all be "bred in the purple" and, if old enough, trained for the job. Still, things can happen in the heat of the auction that cause you to make the wrong choice. Let cooler heads prevail; take a friend or your trainer with you and sit on your

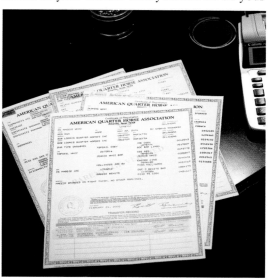

Undoubtedly, most good reining horses come with a set of papers from one of the major performance horse registries, such as the American Quarter or Paint Horse associations.

While it's difficult to look into a crystal ball and tell whether a foal will turn into a top-notch reiner, it's a lot better bet if the young horse comes from a reputable reining horse breeding program.

Looking for a trained reiner or good futurity prospect? Try any of the sales that take place during a major NRHA event.

With a balanced body and structural correctness, this equine athlete looks every inch the part.

hands until you all agree that the "hip number" you're looking at is the right one for you.

One good piece of advice: If you're just beginning in the sport, don't buy the first or most expensive horse you can find right off the bat. Find one that's been successful in the show pen — one that will give you the confidence you need to compete. After you learn "the ropes" from that seasoned horse, then buy one that can help you win a world championship or a major event.

And realize that despite doing everything right — dealing with reputable trainers and breeders and checking out all the best places — you just might fail, not once, but many times in finding the right horse. It's hard and sometimes it's just luck that guides a person in the right direction. Some well-known people in the reining horse industry have been training and/or breeding for the "right" horse for decades and still have never had an NRHA Futurity winner.

Finding a Futurity Prospect

Much of the same philosophy applies if you're hunting a futurity prospect for yourself or one that you intend to hand over to

A horse with wide-set eyes can see well peripherally. They also usually make for an attractive head.

A clean throatlatch allows a horse to flex easily at the poll.

a professional. In the latter case, ask him or her for advice. Don't just go to the local auction and pick out the prettiest horse in the sale, especially if you're looking for a futurity prospect. You don't want to invest your children's college fund on a horse with no proven reining pedigree.

And if you've settled on a trainer you like and want him to ride a futurity prospect for you, ask him what kind of horse he wants to ride. Don't buy something and hope he'll ride it for you. One of the most common mistakes you can make is buying a horse to take to a specific trainer and finding out that the two don't match. It doesn't mean that the horse won't work with another trainer, but if you have your heart set on using that horse trainer, you just might be out of luck. Top pros often have their favorite bloodlines, and you'd be wise to pay attention to that fact.

Also, when looking at any futurity prospect, look hard at the dam's side. Most of the big futurity winners had great mothers. If you have a great broodmare, breed her to the best stallion you can afford.

Equine Athletes

Look at athletes in any human sport. What's the one thing they all have in common, no matter what they do? They all have great bodies. Their arms, legs and torsos are in proportion and suitable for the sport they perform. Their muscles are all in the right places. Even more, their brains are highly engaged and focused and their eye-hand coordination keeps them at the very top of the game in which they excel.

It's the same for equine athletes. They must have the body and brains to do what they do. Reining is an extremely demanding sport on a horse and he needs every advantage if he's to perform successfully in competition where half-points spell the difference between winning and losing fame and fortune.

Here's what to look for in an equine athlete.

Let's start from the top and work our way down. A pretty-headed horse is always going to attract more attention and be more pleasing to look at than a plain-headed one. While having a pretty head doesn't necessarily impact how the horse performs, it adds to the overall impression that the horse is of high quality.

Pretty heads are usually good heads. That means there's width between the eyes, leaving plenty of room for an intelligent brain. Big eyes should be set on the corners of his head, so a horse can see peripherally. Nostrils should be large, allowing the horse to breathe deeply, something he'll need to do as he gallops through a reining pattern.

How the head attaches to the neck is important because it affects the horse's ability to respond to bit pressure. When you pick up on the reins and ask your horse to give to

A horse with a level head and neck-set is easy to keep in frame at any speed.

bit pressure, you want him to be able to bend or flex at the poll, and he can't do that if his head and neck conformation get in the way. You often hear the term "clean throatlatch," which means the throatlatch area isn't thick or coarse. There's a clean line (or plenty of space) from the horse's jawbone to the underside of his neck. That space allows the horse to flex at the poll. If his throatlatch were thick, he couldn't bend well at all, and it might even crimp his air supply, since the horse's trachea or windpipe runs through that same general area. When you hear riders say they like a horse to "bridle well," it means the horse flexes easily at the poll.

Where the neck comes out of the shoulders dictates how a horse carries his head. The "look" you want to present in the show ring is a horse with a level top line from his head to his tail. For this to happen naturally, the neck should come out of the middle of the shoulders. If it sits too high on the shoulders, the horse tends to be high-headed. If it comes out toward the bottom, the horse will be ewe-necked, meaning his neck appears upside down. Neither is attractive in a reining horse.

A horse with level head and neck conformation usually moves his body in a level frame naturally, and you, as the rider, won't have to do much, if anything, to change him. That makes everything in training so much easier.

Shoulders should slope well, in other words, not be too steeply angled. You can determine the slope of a horse's shoulder by drawing an imaginary line from the point of the withers (see below) to the point of the shoulders. It should be about 45 degrees.

There's no substitute for good legs on a horse. They should be well-conformed and have good bone (measuring at least 7 inches around below the knee) to take the stress of training. Horses with fine-boned legs and tiny feet just don't hold up well to the demands of rigorous training.

A good hoof is round (larger at the bottom than at the coronet band), with some depth to the heel and concavity in the sole. The walls are made of solid hoof horn, the bars are pronounced and the frog is V-shaped, thick and rubbery.

Straight legs are a must, although some very athletic horses get by with less than perfect ones. When viewed from the front, you should be able to draw a straight line from the point of the shoulder to the ground,

dissecting the front leg in two — through the forearm, knee, cannon, fetlock and hoof. When viewed from the side, you can draw the same straight line from the middle of the shoulder down through the forearm to the ground. The line should touch the heel bulb.

Use a straight line on hind legs, as well. When viewing the hindquarters from the rear, draw the line from the point of the buttocks down through the middle of the gaskin, hock, cannon, fetlock and hoof. When viewed from the side, the straight line should drop from the point of the buttock and be parallel to the cannon bone on its way down to the ground.

Horses with crooked legs are at risk of injury down the road in training. It doesn't mean they can't do their job; it's that the crooked leg column puts undue stress on the tendons, ligaments and bones, often causing unsoundness.

The front legs should come out of the middle of the horse's shoulders and the hind legs out of the middle of the hindquarters. If they're situated too far forward or back of the midline, the horse won't stand as balanced on his legs. A poorly balanced horse has a much harder time performing demanding reining maneuvers.

A V-shaped chest (muscling between the front legs forms an upside down letter "V") tends to help a horse in the turnarounds. A horse with a flat or thick chest just can't move his legs across his body as efficiently.

Having good head, neck and leg conformation is just part of the performance equation for any horse. His body also contributes to his overall athleticism. A well-balanced equine body takes the shape of a balanced trapezoid

This horse's body exhibits a short back, long underline and matching shoulder and hip angles.

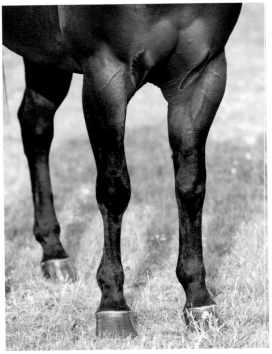

Good legs are straight and have sufficient bone to withstand the rigors of training and performing.

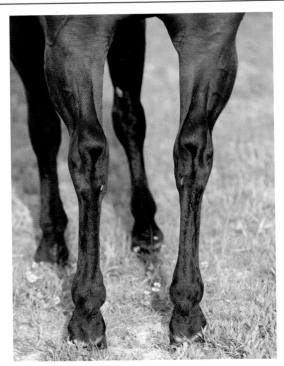

Sturdy hind legs with plenty of gaskin muscling provide the power and strength for sliding stops.

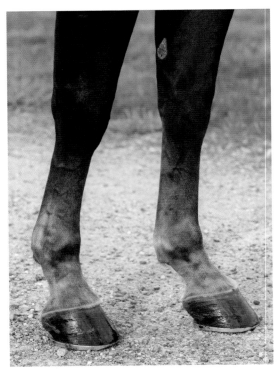

Good legs and feet are important for an equine athlete.

in which the top and bottom sides (back and underline) are parallel and the sides (shoulders and hindquarters) have equal angles. In short, a balanced horse has a short back, long underline and matching shoulder and hip angles. Mismatched angles, such as a 45-degree shoulder and a 60-degree hip, just can't deliver the power that matching angles provide.

A strong, straight back starts off with a good set of withers (point where the neck and back meet), which, ideally, should be level with or above the point of the hip. Otherwise, a horse has "downhill" conformation, meaning his hips are the highest point on his back. While this isn't a major conformational fault, it's not as balanced as a horse with prominent withers. Also, withers help to hold a saddle in place.

A deep heart-girth indicates good wind power, which a reining horse needs to complete the strenuous NRHA patterns. The heart-girth is measured from just behind the withers to the bottom of the barrel. A deep one means there's plenty of room for the horse's heart and lungs.

Look for long, smooth muscling over the body and down the legs, rather than the chunky, oversized muscling so often seen on halter horses. As a human athlete equivalent, think of a gymnast versus a weight lifter or body builder. The gymnast has all the muscles he needs to perform intricate maneuvers demanding agility and strength, yet they don't get in his way. Despite all his strength with his bulky muscles, there's no possibility a body builder would ever be able to execute an "iron cross" on the rings or a double back flip on the pommel horse.

Heart and Desire

Conformation is important in keeping the horse sound, but it's the heart and desire you really ride. We've had some horses that weren't perfectly conformed, and when you look at them, you wonder how they were able to do what they did. It all comes down to heart and desire. If the horse has a big enough heart to try hard and the desire to give you his best performance, then you'll be mounted on a winner.

A good horse has the intelligence to learn quickly and a mindset that accepts training easily. It's okay if he's a little challenging at times, especially in catching on to complicated concepts and maneuvers, but he shouldn't fight the training process.

We've had horses that didn't have the most perfect conformation or even abundant talent, but their brains allowed us to train them to become successful reining horses. We've also had horses with all the ability in the world but no brains, or their personalities got in the way of training. Those are the hardest to give up on because of all their talent, but ultimately they don't make good show horses.

And then there are those who accept the training quickly and, after you take them to their first show, figure out they don't want to be there and find a way to cheat you.

Unlike conformation, heart and desire are intangible assets; but like conformation, they're bred into a horse. He gets his heart and desire from his parents, so breeding horses that were successful show horses is one fairly good way to make sure the heart and desire are there when you need them – on the training track or in the show pen.

You can't tell how much heart and desire a horse has by just looking him. Look at the horse's pedigree and check out his parents' show records if you want to gaze into a crystal ball and foretell what a young prospect might ride like a few years down the road.

A horse's heart and desire are evident in the show ring.

It's not guaranteed, but at least you have a pretty good picture of what to expect.

Certainly, there have been horses that gifted trainers have been able to extract great, futurity-winning performances out of, but it took an arsenal of tricks and a ton of talent on the trainer's part to do it. It seems those horses (if they were stallions or mares) never really reproduced anything that ever wound up in the show pen. The ability was there, but the heart and desire were missing.

A horse with a big heart gives his all to you. He holds nothing back; he's 100 percent show horse. And heart allows him to keep showing, year after year, under any conditions.

"There's no substitute for quality health and hoof care."

3

MAINTAINING THE REINER

The best way to keep your reining horse going strong and competing at a high level is to take very good care of him. There's no substitute for quality health care and hoof care, and without them, your horse can't perform to his potential.

Maintaining a reining horse isn't much different than taking care of any show or performance horse, with the obvious exception of the sport's special shoeing requirements. Effective feed, grooming, veterinary and shoeing programs are a must.

Just as in our training program, we like to keep things simple in all aspects of our health care program. We stay up-to-date with the latest equine health care innovations, certainly, but, for the most part, we stick with the tried-and-true basics of good horsemanship.

It's best to use the services of a shoer knowledgeable in the art of shoeing reining horses. Pictured is Wade Cappel, Sanger, Texas.

TRAINER'S TIPS

Shawn's Feeding Program

Shawn feeds a 13-percent protein commercial sweet-feed grain mix and a grass/alfalfa-mix hay three times a day – split between breakfast, dinner and 9:00 at night to 3-year-old futurity horses. Older horses just get hay twice a day, unless they're thin.

He keeps the same routine at horse shows.

TRAINER'S TIPS

Craig's Feeding Program

Craig feeds quality alfalfa hay and alfalfa pellets and a commercial high-performance feed (nutrient-dense pellets or extruded nuggets balanced for protein, fat, fiber, vitamins and minerals) and/or a stabilized rice bran product to the horses in competition or those that need more than just hay.

He feeds twice a day, but enough at a time so there's hay in the feeder all day long. Basically, it's free-choice hay. Easy keepers get less so they don't get fat.

To keep horses busy and not bored at horse shows, he throws them a grass-alfalfa "sandwich," placing the grass in between two flakes of alfalfa.

Feed

When it comes to feeding your horse, our best advice is to buy the best you can. It's the cheapest insurance you can have when it comes to your horse's continued good health.

Feeding programs differ all over the country, depending on available forage, and ours differ from one another (see sidebars). Work with your veterinarian or an equine nutritionist to balance your horse's diet, making sure he has all the necessary nutrients, vitamins and minerals.

However, no matter where you live or your situation, hay should be the mainstay of your horse's diet. Buy your supply from a reputable dealer to ensure that you get a consistently good product.

What's vitally important is to feed hay often and enough. Horses evolved as grazing animals and were designed to forage throughout the day. It's best to try to do whatever you can to mimic what's natural for them. You'll have a lot fewer sick horses if you do.

Keeping high-quality hay in front of stall-bound horses also helps alleviate boredom.

Another suggestion is to feed hay at ground level, which again is more natural for the horse.

Ground-level feeders allow horses to eat from a natural head-down position. Automatic waterers are in the opposite corner of the stalls.

Hay should be the mainstay of a horse's diet. Here, premium-grade alfalfa is being tossed to broodmares.

Either place the feed on the stall floor or in ground-level feeders that allow the horse to put his head down, as in the act of grazing. It's been proven that when a horse holds his head in this position, his digestive juices come into play and help process his feed more efficiently.

It should go without saying that the horse needs clean, fresh water at all times. If you have automatic waterers, clean them regularly. If you have to fill your bucket from a hose, think of some way to take off the chill in winter, such as with bucket heaters. Horses will drink more if the water isn't ice cold. Without adequate water, no horse can digest his feed properly and that provides the right environment for more colic cases.

Grooming

Grooming plays a huge part in your show-ring presentation. A horse with long hair and a dull coat gives the judge the wrong impression and speaks volumes about your lack of care. Remember, you're trying to make a good first impression the second you step into the arena, so presenting a horse with a shiny coat and long, flowing mane and tail has to help. For that to happen, you'll have to pay close attention to your grooming program all year long.

In addition to providing high-quality feed for healthy coat condition, the standard method for keeping a haircoat short and shiny is to blanket your horse 15 hours a day, starting Sept. 1 through May 1, from 6:00 p.m. to 10:00 a.m. As soon as it feels cool, blanket. Depending on your stabling facilities and the weather, you might consider putting a hood on your horse as well.

For a slick and shiny haircoat in the summer, use a lightweight sheet or a fly sheet on your horse to help prevent his coat from fading in the sun when you turn him out for exercise.

After every workout, rinse your horse to remove the sweat. The all-in-one bathing solutions that come premixed in a container are handy to use. If it's too cold for a water rinse, then vacuum your horse.

For the best results with manes and tails, shampoo and condition them once a week. There are a couple of ways to maintain them on a daily basis, and much depends on the stall environment and barn equipment you have as to which one you want to use.

One method is to simply keep them clean and untangled. Use a wide-tooth comb when you do brush through either the mane or the tail. The wide teeth work through snags, but don't tear out the hair as much. Hold the section of hair you're working on as you comb through the strands from top to bottom.

The other method is to braid the tail in a simple three-plait braid. Intertwine the plaits snugly, but not tight, and don't plait them every day or you'll break off hair.

Three-plait braiding is a common way to keep tails in good condition.

Blankets are a fact of life for all show horses.

TRAINER'S TIPS

Craig's Turnout and Exercise Program

Horses in Craig's barn get turned out a couple of times a week in shady paddocks, with safe fencing.

He also puts them on a motorized round-pen exerciser, which has divided compartments for six head of horses. Unlike a hot walker that can put a horse's head at an unnatural angle, the motorized round pen allows the horse to be untied and move freely. Also, it can be programmed at different speeds, causing the horse to either walk fast, trot or lope.

The exerciser is especially helpful on Monday mornings when horses, especially young ones, are full of energy after a day or two off and like to run and buck. When they're through, they're ready to work. It's better than chasing them around in a round pen; horses exercise themselves naturally.

Giving a horse free time in a pasture or paddock provides him a mental and physical break from living in a box stall. A note with respect to grooming: This horse's impossibly long mane is kept tangle-free by regular washing and conditioning.

You can further protect a braided tail by putting it in a sock or tail bag, but beware. They can get caught on water buckets or other stall equipment and rip out. If your bucket rests on a hook, cover the hook with tape so it can't snag braided hair. Better yet, put your bucket in brackets or hang it on some form of smooth clip or carabiner.

To prevent your horse from stepping on his tail when he backs, keep the sock or bag on all the time, even while riding. Or you can blunt cut the bottom of the tail, keeping it several inches off the ground.

Leg Protection

When riding or training your horse, always use protective leg gear to help prevent any injuries (see chapter titled "Tack and Equipment"). As a rule, you should have splint or sports medicine-type boots on the front legs at all times while riding. For extra protection and especially for a horse that overreaches (hind feet clip the front feet), you might consider bell boots if they're not incorporated into the splint-boot design. Also, if your horse tends to hit his knees, try using knee boots as well.

While your horse should wear front-leg protection whenever you ride, use skid boots on his hind fetlocks only when you ask him to stop hard. Otherwise, leave them off. You can hang them on the back cinch or on a back D-ring, step off your horse and put them on just before you practice stopping. Riding with them on all the time can possibly cause some chafing, so just use them when you need them.

Also, if your horse has burned his hocks stopping and/or is a very deep stopper, you might consider putting hock boots on him as well, but just during stopping practice.

A round-pen exerciser with separate compartments permits horses to move freely at various gaits without being tied, unlike the traditional hot-walker.

Leg protection is a must for any reining workout.

Let a hot and sweaty horse rest to catch his breath and cool down.

Using water or ice-therapy boots is an excellent way to tighten tired tendons after practice.

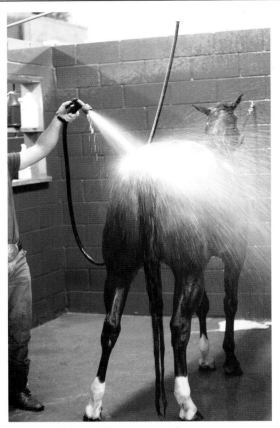

Rinsing a horse after every workout removes sweat and dirt.

Cool Down

After a particularly hard workout, or any practice session, for that matter, always cool down your horse physically by walking him around until his breathing has returned to normal and he's relaxed. Then, rinse off his body to cool him and get rid of any sweat marks. Never put a hot and sweaty horse back in his stall. His body worked overtime during practice and needs time to recuperate before being stuck back in a box stall.

Legs undergo a lot of stress when performing reining maneuvers and need special care. Cooling them down, either the old-fashioned way with a cold-water hosing or with specialized equipment, is a necessary part of reining-horse maintenance. Ice-wraps, whirlpool boots and high-tech water and/or ice therapy machines are worth their money, not only in saving you time and effort, but in your horse's health and longevity. While cooldown therapies and gadgets are great, don't depend upon them to always do the trick when you ride a horse hard.

The real secret to keeping your horse's legs sound and healthy is to have a consistent training program, not one that's hit or miss. In other words, don't let your horse stand in his stall for five days and then work him hard on the sixth. That's a recipe for torn tendons. The best way to keep your horse's tendons and ligaments tight is to not overwork them excessively in the first place. You've got to know when to quit in any practice session. When a horse is done, he's done, and if you keep working him — asking for one more stop, one more turnaround — you take the risk of pulling a ligament or blowing a tendon. Your horse will be months in rehab and possibly never come back. Once a tendon or ligament goes, it's difficult and sometimes impossible to return it to its former healthy condition.

Horses today are bred to keep going; they have the heart and desire to work till they drop. It's up to you to determine when your horse has had enough. Are his sides heaving, nostrils flaring? Are sweat and foam dripping off his body? Then quit for the day, or better yet, quit before he gets to that point. Cool him out by walking him slowly until his body returns to normal, then cool down his legs and put him away.

Shoes should be shaped to fit the horse's feet. Anvil work can help.

If, after a workout, your horse seems a little stiff or sore or if you're at a show and you think your horse needs extra protection because of the show-grounds stall floors, you can use a leg brace in conjunction with standing polo bandages. That might help tighten tendons and alleviate a potential problem. But don't wrap religiously. It can create a dependency and instead of providing stronger legs it might do just the opposite.

Check It Out

Anytime your horse feels the least bit "off," check him out. A lame horse will walk and even lope soundly, but not trot soundly. Notify your veterinarian immediately and have him or her take care of the problem before it becomes a big one. You never want your horse to associate his work with pain. You want him comfortable at all times.

TRAINER'S TIPS

Craig's Shoeing Program

For the horse that stops narrow, Craig's shoer widens the outside of the slide plate to help the horse spread out. For the horse that stops wide, he widens the inside. The bigger the shoe area, the more drag there is to that side.

To speed the break-over of a horse's front feet, he either rolls the toe or uses aluminum shoes.

He puts eight nails into each slide plate because horses that stop hard with a lot of torque can easily pull off a shoe.

Slide plates made wider on the outside help a horse's feet to spread out during stopping. The reverse is true for the horse that stops wide behind.

Another thing to watch for with regard to pain and potential problems is inconsistency in your horse's performance. If he's been stopping great during practice, but one day he quits, pay attention to what your horse is trying to tell you. He might just be having a bad day, but if he has two or three in a row, then call your vet. Your horse might not be visibly sore or lame, but something is wrong somewhere.

Shoeing

When it comes to horse care, the one thing that really distinguishes our sport from others is that our horses have special shoeing requirements. Slide plates are standard equipment on every reining horse; you can't very well perform the reiner's famous sliding stop without them.

One very important piece of advice: It's best to have a reining horseshoer work on your horses rather than one unfamiliar with the needs of the sport. A farrier who shoes hunter-jumpers or pleasure horses very likely will not know how to shoe a reiner with slide plates.

There are a lot of ways to approach shoeing, but just like feeding and grooming, we keep our program as simple and natural as we can. For example, we leave our horses barefoot in front as long as we can, especially 2-year-olds. That allows the hoofs to spread and grow to the size nature intended for the horse.

Shoeing a young horse too early prevents the hoof capsule from developing as good or as large as it would normally. Sometimes we don't shoe in front until we show the horse for the first time; and sometimes we never shoe them in front. It all depends on the horse and his feet. Some have tougher, harder horn than others that have thinner walls and soles. The local soil conditions also play a part. Some parts of the country are rockier than others. If you ride a horse hard and he appears a little sore, we definitely suggest shoeing him.

There's a saying: Shoe to fit the horse, not the other way around. The horse's hoof shouldn't be trimmed to fit a particular size shoe; the shoe should be shaped to fit the

Slide plates come in various sizes. The wider the shoe, the more slide it creates.

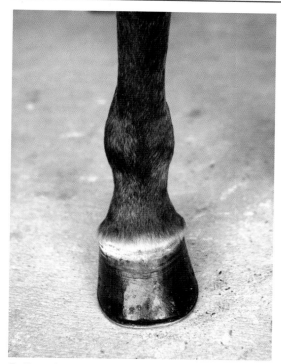

Rolling the toe helps early break-over in the horse's front feet.

TRAINER'S TIPS

Shawn's Shoeing Program

Shawn's shoer (his brother Mark Flarida) fits the horse's front feet as full as possible, meaning to the shape of the hoof. The shoe doesn't crowd or pinch the horse, especially in the heel area. If necessary, he fills in with an acrylic adhesive material designed by NASA to hold shuttle tiles on, much like women's fake fingernails. If the shoe is wider than the foot in spots, he fills the gap with the material to keep the horse from pulling off the shoes.

With thin-walled horses, he sometimes glues on shoes instead of nailing them, and uses only six nails on slide plates. He doesn't reshape slide plates for horses that spread their legs when they slide. Shawn thinks horses find their way eventually and learn to stop straight.

horse's foot. And the horse's feet should be trimmed and shod level as they stand, meaning there's not much you can do to straighten crooked feet, so don't try with special or corrective shoes. Angles in the front and hind feet should be aligned with the horse's fetlocks, not broken backward or forward.

Because a horse's hoofs can grow from ¼- to ½-inch a month, we trim and reset shoes every five weeks, depending on the horse's feet. For example, if a horse grows a lot of toe, he might need more maintenance, say every 30 days.

Slide Plates

Slide plates on the hind feet are the reiner's trademark. They typically are manufactured in different widths (from ¾-inch to 1 ½-inch) or knowledgeable shoers know how to make them. Some horses never get past ¾-inch plates, however. They slide just fine with minimal plate.

We have our horses shod with either ¾-, ⅞- or 1-inch slide plates after the first 30 to 60 days of riding. With ¾-inch plates (often called "baby sliders"), a horse has to put some effort into stopping, more so than with 1-inch plates. The latter are more conducive to sliding; however, be aware that a horse might scare himself the first time the ground slides out from underneath him.

But as soon as a young horse tries to stop and slide, shoe the hind feet to encourage him to slide.

After a young horse is shod with slide plates for the first time, go easy on asking him to stop hard and fast. It's best to allow the horse to become used to the slippery feel of the plates on his hind feet. A green 2-year-old might quit trying to stop if he becomes scared. It might take him awhile to acclimate to the strange sensation. So go slowly and allow the horse to adjust on his own. Don't say "whoa" for a few days after the initial shoeing, just break the horse down to a trot and then stop him. He won't slip as much going at a slower speed.

We very seldom go to more than 1-inch sliders on any of our horses. Horses with plates that are too big often fall down in the large, fast circles or get too far underneath themselves in a stop. A horse that's a big stopper doesn't need to have big plates to stop, as reining horses in the past did. Horses are better athletes today and can really attack the ground. They really, really want to stop, and they don't need a whole lot of shoe to do it. If you put too much plate on them, they get scared and stop stopping. On the other hand, horses without as much try or natural ability need all the slide plate they can get to help them stop.

We communicate with our shoers often about how our horses are riding, how they're running and stopping, so the professional shoer can put the right shoe on the horse and help him in his career as a reiner.

"Think of the dirt in your arena or on your slide track as an important training tool."

4

GOOD GROUND

Training on good ground is essential for any performance horse, but the right kind of ground is especially important for the reiner. Think of the dirt in your arena or on your slide track (or that of your trainer's) as an important tool to get your job done successfully. It either helps or hinders your training, and it can seriously affect your horse's soundness. For example, hard ground can bruise your horse's soles, particularly on the front feet. Overly deep ground can cause your horse to be at risk for suspensory, stifle and hock injuries.

We're adamant about the kind of dirt we work our horses on. It has to be in tip-top shape at all times, and we constantly maintain it throughout the day to keep it that way. In this chapter, we'll discuss what good ground conditions are and how you, too, can approach that in your own situation.

The information in this chapter was gleaned from the industry's top expert in arena consulting and construction, Bob Kiser of Kiser Arena Specialists™, Gainesville, Texas (www.kiserproducts.com). Bob has been responsible for dirt at the NRHA's major events since they debuted at the Oklahoma City Fairgrounds in the mid-1980s. He's now in demand worldwide to help create the surfaces for international-level reining competition. We're grateful to Bob for lending us his time and talent for this book.

Ground Has Changed

In the last 20 years or so, reining horse ground has changed dramatically, right along with the horses.

Years ago everybody thought you had to have a rock-hard clay base with pure sand on top to slide. They thought it had to be real smooth and slick or horses wouldn't stop. But all that did was produce a lot of sore and crippled horses. We've proved that that type of surface isn't the best option for reining horses and here's why.

Modern reining horses have evolved into superb athletes. They're a lot bigger stoppers, and the old-type ground doesn't work as well for them. There's nothing in the old ground for today's horse to get ahold of. If he hit the hard, slick base, he'd get scared.

The only way to adjust how a horse stops is by the depth of the sand. Unfortunately, sand creates a surface that becomes very uneven very quickly. When horses stop in sand, they push it forward and make mounds. The arena ends up with a mixture of thin and heavy spots.

The dirt you ride on is vitally important to your training efforts and to the soundness of your horse.

Also, a horse tends to slip in big, fast circles on that type of ground because sand has no stability to it. It gives way underneath a horse's hoofs.

By the time the 10th horse runs in a reining, there'd be no good ground to run on. They'd slip and fall out of lead, etc. In the past, it became very critical for competitors to find new ground to stop on after a few horses went.

In my experience working with the NRHA's major events, I tested lots of soils and started mixing silt and clay into sand to give it more stability. As I learned how to do that, I perfected a material that actually doesn't have a base, and that's the way most of the top reining horse arenas are built today. We use material that's pretty much the same from the bottom to the top. There's no base, and the type of sand and clay mix that we use tends to flow around the horse's hoof in a stop rather than push ahead of it.

The OKC arena dirt is made up of about 85 percent sand and 15 percent silt and clay. It's an extremely fine sand, which is what makes it work.

In this type of material, horses find the level that allows them to stop best. The really powerful stoppers, the ones that attack the

ground, go deep into the material. The skaters that stand up to stop can slide a long way, but they stay shallow on top of the ground. It works for either stopping style.

Types of Soil

Basically there are three classifications of soil material: sand (large particle), silt and clay, which is the smallest of the three types of soil. Silt is basically a little bit bigger particle of clay.

Each area of the country has its own type of soil and you have to work with what you've got. There is no single standard people can use nationwide to make good arena ground. What's available in California is different than what's in Texas and that's different from Florida.

Some areas of the country, such as the Southwest and Rocky Mountain states, have decomposed granite. This material can work well in a reining horse arena, but it's really abrasive and can be hard underneath. People in that part of the country must find other types of material to add to their soil, such as fine sand, to take a little bit of the abrasiveness out of it.

The ideal material for reining horse arenas is a sandy loam mixture (clay mixed with fine sand). But just as with soil, there are no

The arena dirt at the NRHA's major events has been groomed by Kiser Arena Specialists since the mid-1980s.

The best type of footing for reining arenas is a mixture of clay and sand.

Choose a level site for your slide track or arena. The less grader work you have to do, the better.

standards for types of sand across the country. If you ask for concrete sand in Ohio, it'll be different than the concrete sand available in New Mexico. Typically, concrete sand has a wider variation in size than masonry sand. Look for masonry sand to mix in with your soil. It's finer and more uniform. Concrete sand might have small stones in it. Coarse sand is too abrasive on a horse's legs and feet. If it gets under the skid or splint boots, it'll really rub a horse raw.

Also, fine sand is more stable. It doesn't move as much under a horse's hoof. Coarse sand "rolls" underneath a horse. If he's pushing in a circle, it'll actually roll with his feet and make him slip.

Sand wears out. Even though it's an extremely hard particle, it'll break in two. Horses' hoofs are hard on sand. A 1,200-pound horse at a full gallop exerts 1,400 pounds per square inch when he hits the ground. When horses ride on sand, they break down the sand particles so fine they begin to pack. When you hear people say their "ground is worn out," that's what they mean. The sand becomes finer and finer until a certain amount of it turns to dust. That's why an older arena is dustier than a new one.

Your arena won't wear out as fast as a professional trainer's arena will. Most pros have to add sand once a year. You might not have to for five or six years. Then, all you'll probably need is to add a half inch and your surface will be good to go again.

If all you have to work with is clay, add sand to it. How much depends on the type of clay; it's impossible to give exact percentages. Mix until you create a sandy loam material that has some cushion to it and drains well.

A deep sand arena is as damaging on a horse as a hard clay base, maybe worse. Deep sand has no bottom to it or rebound. To remain sound over time, your horse's feet need

The dirt in indoor or covered arenas doesn't face the same weather challenges as that of outdoor arenas.

to hit the ground and spring back from it. An analogy: think of a wood floor and a concrete floor. The wood has some give to it, whereas the concrete doesn't. A sandy loam mixture provides the safest surface for riding reiners.

Site Selection and Preparation

Selecting a good arena site is crucial. The first thing to look for is soil type, one that mixes well with sand.

Next, if you're building an outdoor arena, pick the highest spot for good drainage. An indoor arena doesn't have the same challenges because it's in the same environment every day. But an outdoor arena constantly goes through weather changes.

Down time after a rainfall can mean anywhere from one afternoon caused by light rain to days from a downpour. You might not be able to afford that much time off if you're getting ready for a competition.

Drainage is a huge factor. There are lots of cases where if the person had moved the arena just 100 feet farther away, he would've had a better drained arena, but instead he moved it closer to the barn for convenience.

Slope the arena from one long side to the other, about a 1 percent slope from edge to edge.

For ground that has a real tight soil that doesn't drain well, slope the arena 1 foot from end to opposite end. It would be a foot higher on one end than the other. If you have a subsoil that percolates water well, you can get by with less, say 9 to 10 inches.

When you do less, say 6 inches, if the ground isn't dragged real well, you'll have spots in the arena where water will collect and stand.

Unfortunately, everything that has an upside has a downside. If your slope is around 1 percent or a foot and you have a hard, driving rain that falls an inch an hour or more, you might have quite a bit of erosion of material along the sloped or downside.

You can drain the arena internally by laying 3- or 4-inch diameter drain tile (black, corrugated plastic with slits in them that comes in big rolls, found at places like Home Depot) from one end to the opposite end and lay gravel on top of it. Lay it deep enough so you don't rake it up when you drag. When water goes through the top material, it filters into the tile and drains out.

You can also tie the lines with a 6-inch main line along the lower end. It'll drain all the water out the bottom corner of the arena. The fall from the top to the bottom of the arena has to be only about 2 inches, just enough for the water to run downhill.

Another reason to not use pure sand is that sand will filter into the drain tile slits and

After trial and error, you'll know just how dry or moist your arena dirt should be.

A drag that incorporates a watering system is the best for working reining arenas.

Professional reining horse trainers work their slide tracks several times a day.

clog them. There's drain tile that has a sand sock over it on the market. It's a nylon sleeve that won't let sand in.

Look at the slope of your land. A good fall-off should be obvious. If at all possible, avoid building in a place where you have to change the elevation of the land to accommodate your arena. Cutting into land for a level place to ride isn't so bad; it's when you have to add fill dirt that the problem arises.

The land cut into will stay solid under your horse's feet, but the filled-in portion might not be as stable. The trick is getting it packed enough because it'll settle after a time. Therefore, it'll always be hard to get your ground on the fill side as good as the cut side.

If you can hire someone who's good at road construction they can do that, but it's critical that it get done properly or you'll continually have problems with the level and depth of your ground from one side to the next.

If you can afford to do it, it's good to have soil engineers come to test the compaction between both the cut and the fill sides. They'll take a soil sample and tell you what the maximum compaction rate should be.

It's best not to "crown" your arena; that is, don't slope the arena from the center outward in an effort to improve drainage. What happens is this: If you put a 1 percent slope in the middle, any good arena drag will take the crown right off of it. If it does, then you have a flat arena that doesn't drain at all.

The other thing that happens when you crown an arena is that the base material is crowned as well. So when you drag and flatten it, then the crowned middle gets thin and hard. The outer edges of the arena have 4 inches or more of material and the center has an inch. Then you start cutting into your base material.

Weather Considerations

Typically, it doesn't matter what direction you orient your arena with the exception of one weather element — the wind. All parts of the country have prevailing winds. The wind typically comes from one direction on a consistent basis, and you should find out what that is.

Avoid orienting the long side of your arena toward the prevailing winds. For example, if your arena is 150 by 300 feet and your prevailing winds come from the southwest, don't have your long side, or the

TRAINER'S TIP

Arena Size

A good size is 130 by 260 feet, and 150 by 300 feet is even better. The former is a nice size for most arenas. Arenas that are too small, say 100 by 200 feet, don't provide enough room to complete maneuvers.

They're too narrow and too short. If you get a horse running fast, you run out of arena too soon to stop well.

300-foot side, face the southwest. Over time, the prevailing winds will carry your material away. Wind erosion isn't as immediately damaging as water erosion, but it still plays a part in the long-term condition of your arena. So, plan for it in the beginning, just like drainage, and you'll be better off in the long run.

Lay out the long side of your arena perpendicular to the wind to avoid these problems.

This isn't a huge issue and sometimes it's not possible to design the arena around it, but give it some thought if you can. It's the same as building a barn in hot climates. It makes sense to orient the doors in the direction of the wind to bring breezes into hot stalls. In cold climates, you'd want just the opposite.

Rocks

One of the biggest arena problems you find in any part of the country is rocks. Finding sand or soil without rocks in it is almost impossible, whether it's in California or Vermont. No matter how many times you drag and keep the rocks picked up, they keep popping up to the surface.

You can lay a road filter fabric over the ground after the excavation and leveling are done so the rocks don't come up. Then put arena material over the top of it.

However, you'd better put enough material on top of the fabric so you'll never get to it with your arena drag. If you ever hook it, you've got a real train wreck.

Filter fabric is used on roads because it stabilizes the soil as well as keeps rocks from coming up. It can be purchased from road construction companies, or they know of sources for it. It comes in huge rolls – usually 60 feet wide and 400 or 500 feet long.

It's a good option, not only for rocks, but for any unstable soil. It helps bind the top material to the subsoil.

Riding horses across the pasture or in rougher country teaches them to handle themselves on all types of ground, something a perfectly manicured arena can't do.

Moisture

Moisture is very critical in a reining horse arena. Water is beneficial for more than dust control. It takes up the space between the soil particles, and that's what makes the cushion. When you lose the moisture, the soil becomes flat. There's nothing to take up the space. Notice, if your arena is typically 2 inches deep and it gets really dry, it might be only 1 ½ inches deep. When you water it, it's 2 inches deep again.

For a good cushion, the moisture content of the soil should be between 4 and 7 percent. There's only one accurate way to measure that. There's no inexpensive and adequate moisture sensor on the market, but you can measure the moisture effectively with a microwave oven.

Dig up a soil sample when it appears to be the correct moisture and put it into a plastic or microwave-safe container. Weigh it on a postage scale, which can be purchased at office supply stores. You'll get a measurement in grams; a scale that measures ounces works too, but it won't be as accurate as in grams.

Then dry it in the microwave for 3 minutes at a time. Take the soil out and stir it. It might take several tries to dry out the soil sufficiently, depending on how wet the dirt is. Like most microwave ovens, it'll "cook" the edges first. Therefore, you'll have to mix up the soil so it dries throughout. Weigh it again. Divide the wet weight into the dry weight and you get the percentage of moisture content.

For example, if the dirt weighs 500 grams wet and 465 grams when it's dry, divide 465 by 500 and you'll get .93. Subtract .93 from 1.00 and that equals 7 percent moisture. It should be somewhere between 4 and 7 percent.

After you've weighed your dirt a time or two, you'll figure out what ideal dirt feels and looks like and you can water your arena accordingly. You shouldn't have to weigh it after that.

As a rule of thumb, any time you start seeing dust in an arena, it's probably too dry and needs watering.

Watering the Arena

The best way to work an arena is with a drag that incorporates a watering system. That way you can apply water in even, precise amounts, and the entire arena is treated equally.

However, if you don't have such a drag, the next best thing is to get a water tank on a trailer that you can drag behind your pickup. You must have some way to control the amount of water you spread on your ground.

The worst thing you can do is water with a garden hose or with a movable sprinkler. You just can't tell how much went where. You'll have uneven spots throughout your arena. Some parts will be wet and heavy and others lighter and drier. When you run circles or stop, your horse won't have consistent ground to work on, and possibly end up with injuries.

Work the Arena

To do a good job on a reining arena, you really need a medium-size tractor to pull the drag, one with at least 35 horsepower.

The drag has to be capable of grooming the soil at a uniform depth every single time. Whether the depth is 1 inch or 2, it must work the ground uniformly. Some inexpensive drags don't do that, so you're better off paying the extra price for a good one.

The drag has to be able to work the whole soil profile down to the bottom or where you want to stop. It shouldn't have huge teeth that simply dig up the ground. It should cut the soil profile down to a specified depth. If it doesn't, you'll get hard spots and then you start crippling horses.

As a rule of thumb, if you ride two horses a day on an arena, it should be worked (watered and dragged) every day, even if you ride each horse for only 45 minutes apiece.

Some professional trainers work their arenas three times a day, but then they ride dozens of horses daily. They realize the importance of keeping the ground consistent all day long.

Balancing Act

A horse gets used to the ground on which he's trained. If it's deep, he'll develop a way to go in it and be comfortable; the same thing with shallow ground. It's when he goes to different kinds of dirt that he finds himself unsure of his footing. Because he won't move normally on the strange surface, he might compensate for the conditions and possibly end up with lameness problems.

People try to mimic the ground at the NRHA Futurity at home and that's all well and good. However, when you ride on perfect ground all the time, a horse doesn't learn how to balance himself in bad ground. It's a good idea to ride your horse around the pasture or in rougher country so he can learn to handle himself in a variety of ground conditions. A lot of natural balance or self-carriage tends to get lost in show horses that go from perfectly groomed stalls to perfectly groomed arenas. So, take your horse trail riding, on safe ground, of course.

"Without good tools, you can't do a good job."

5

TACK AND EQUIPMENT

Tack and equipment are the tools of the horseman's trade, and without good tools, you can't do a good job.

Be very particular about your gear. You want it well-made and comfortable for both you and your horse. It won't work if, when you're trying to get across a complicated maneuver to your horse, he's distracted and maybe in pain from a too-tight bit or poor-fitting saddle.

In this chapter, we'll explain the tools we use to get our job done and how we use them.

Snaffle Bits

The snaffle bit is typically the first bit to use when starting a young horse, and it's also an excellent choice for re-schooling an older horse.

Snaffles are simple bits that consist of a mouthpiece (usually broken or jointed) and bit rings. There are many configurations of mouthpieces and rings, but we'll discuss the most common, which also happen to be our favorites.

Snaffle bits work primarily on the corners of the mouth by providing direct pressure from the bit rings to the rider's hands. If you pull the reins with 1 ounce of pressure, the horse feels that 1 ounce. If you pull with 10 pounds, he feels 10 pounds of pressure in his mouth.

Snaffle bits are meant to be ridden two-handed, giving you control over both sides of the horse's face and therefore both sides of his body. When you pull the right rein, it interacts with the right snaffle bit ring, and the horse follows his nose to the right. The same with the left rein.

The rings to which the reins are attached can be either D- or O-shaped. An O-ring is the traditional snaffle bit configuration. It's often called a loose-ring, because the cheek pieces slide freely through the butt ends of the mouthpiece. On it, reins can travel (slide) the length of the O when you apply rein pressure. Therefore, the "signal" from the bit takes a little bit of time before it gets to the horse's mouth. This gives your horse time to respond when he feels you pick up the reins.

The D-ring is shaped as the letter "D" with one long side and a semi-circle. Because of this fixed shape, the reins are more stationary. Therefore, the bit signal is quicker because the reins can't travel any farther than the long side of the D. The D-shape also helps prevent the bit from pinching the horse's lips, a potential problem with an O-ring.

Using high quality tack is the mark of a true horseman. Here's a braided rawhide split-ear headstall suitable for everyday use as well as show.

Most snaffles have jointed mouthpieces, usually made of smooth cold-rolled steel or iron, sometimes inlaid with copper, which helps a horse to salivate, therefore keeping a moist mouth. Stainless steel is another type of metal often used in bits, but horses prefer cold-rolled steel or iron.

Typically, the diameter of a mild snaffle bit is around $3/8$ of an inch. Thinner mouthpieces on snaffles (and on curb bits, see below) are harsher than medium to thick mouthpieces because there's more "bite" on the surface of the horse's tongue when the mouthpiece diameter is small.

You can keep your horse in a smooth snaffle for three or four months until the horse gets used to it, or longer if he's comfortable and going well for you. When he starts to lean on it, change to a twisted-wire snaffle. Its mouthpiece barrel is twisted, thereby creating more of a biting edge. Horses respect it more than a smooth barrel mouthpiece. Stick with medium-sized twisted wire mouthpieces. There are thin twisted wires, but they're too severe.

A snaffle bit is a nice bit to drive a young horse up into when teaching him to give to bit pressure. The horse runs into the imaginary wall made by the bit and gives to the pressure by bending or "breaking" at the poll. We often refer to it as being "soft" or "broke in the face."

It's a good idea to put a leather curb strap on all snaffle bits. The strap has no actual bit function, but it helps prevent the bit from running through a horse's mouth at the pull on the reins.

As for fit, whether a snaffle or a curb bit, adjust it to fit comfortably with no wrinkles at the corners of the horse's mouth. The bit should rest across the mouth bars in the interdental space between the incisors and the molars. Adjusting the bit too tightly will pinch the horse and having it too loose might cause the mouthpiece to constantly hit the horse's incisors. Both situations are painful and irritating. Your horse won't be able to pay attention to you if he's distracted by the pain in his mouth.

A snaffle bit, such as this O-ring, provides direct contact between the rider's hands and the horse's mouth. When the rider pulls left, the horse follows the feel to the left. This training bridle is outfitted with a noseband and a German martingale.

Curb Bits

Once your horse gets "soft" in the snaffle (performing all the maneuvers well and on a loose rein), you're ready to advance his education. You further develop his mouth and bit response by graduating to a mild leverage or curb bit. Like snaffle bits, curb bits come in numerous mouthpiece configurations. The big difference is that curb bits have shanks, which create leverage action. Now, instead of a direct pull from the bit rings to the rider's hand, there's a fulcrum effect between the mouthpiece (usually a port), shanks and a chin (or curb) strap.

With a curb bit, your rein pressure is amplified because the leverage is much greater. Instead of the one-to-one ratio (1:1) you have with a snaffle bit, you usually have anywhere from 1:3 (moderate) to 1:7 (severe) with a curb bit. The severity depends on the length of the shanks — the longer, the more severe because there's more leverage pull.

Ports on curb bits allow for tongue relief and aren't as severe as they might look. Most ports don't come into contact with the horse's palate or roof of the mouth unless they're tall, say over 2 ½ inches. Medium ports are by far the most popular for reiners.

The chin or curb strap is made of either leather or chain and attaches to the bit rings. A comfortable size for curb chains is around ½-inch wide. That way the horse has more chain surface to feel. A small curb chain has too much "bite" and could scare a horse. Use a leather chin strap only as a bit hobble on snaffles. However, if you had a horse that is overly reactive to bit pressure, you might use a leather strap on your leverage bit.

On a young horse, say a late 2-year-old or early 3-year-old, start with a loose curb chain, which creates a long bit signal,

An O- or loose-ring snaffle with a medium-sized smooth mouthpiece is typically the first bit used on young horses. Note the leather curb strap, used to prevent the bit rings from being pulled through the horse's mouth.

A D-ring snaffle with a twisted-wire mouthpiece is a good choice when a horse starts leaning on the bit.

The medium-height port on this curb bit provides tongue relief.

This correctional bit has copper barrels to encourage salivation in the horse.

With a properly fitted bit, either snaffle or curb, there should be no wrinkles at the corners of the horse's mouth.

Split-ear headstalls are often used on finished show horses. Pictured is a double split-ear headstall.

Most snaffle bits are attached to browband headstalls. The throatlatch strap keeps the bridle in place should a young horse rub his head.

A noseband encourages a horse to keep its mouth shut.

meaning it takes more time for the bit to engage. The horse learns to carry the bit before you use curb action to its fullest. You can tighten the chain as the horse becomes more used to the curb bit. With any properly adjusted curb chain, you should be able to fit two fingers between the horse's jawbone and the chain.

A mild correctional bit (one with a medium port and medium shanks) is a good choice for young or green horses and actually can be used throughout the rest of the horse's training. However, as with any bit, you can make it as harsh as you want by the use of your hands. The shanks are about 6 to 7 inches long and hang loose (loose-jawed), which gives an independent action to each side of the bit. Also, they have a lot of swing or "signal." This means that when you pull the reins, the shank can swing or sweep back a long way before the chin strap, and therefore leverage, engages and takes effect on the horse's mouth and jawbone.

As an interim bit between the snaffle and curb bits, you can use a jointed-mouthpiece shank bit, often called an Argentine snaffle. Many trainers use this, but about 90 percent of our riding is done in a medium correctional.

Don't be afraid to switch bits on a horse. Your horse might become overly comfortable with one bit and start to lean on it. Try different bits to back him off, thereby keeping his mouth fresh and responsive to you. Don't forget that any bit is only as good as the hands using it; but with that said, your horse should be learning and getting better all the time, not finding ways to avoid your cues. Switching bits can keep him guessing and sharp.

Headstalls

Headstalls come in two basic varieties — browband and split or one-ear.

A browband headstall has a band across the horse's brow connecting the two cheek-pieces, thus the name. There's a throatlatch strap behind the horse's jaw, preventing the horse from rubbing off the headstall. Adjust it so that you can place two fingers between the horse's throatlatch and the strap when the horse holds his head in a normal position. A too-tight throatlatch prevents a horse from being able to bend at the poll effectively and can even interfere with his breathing. A too-loose strap is sloppy looking and possibly ineffective in keeping the headstall in place.

The split- or one-ear headstall is also aptly described in that it has one earpiece that fits over the right ear. There can either be a slit in the crownpiece leather or a sliding loop to contain the ear. Some bridles have two loops, making them double-ear headstalls. Traditionally, but not always, they don't have throatlatch straps to secure them, which makes them better suited for older horses used to "packing" a bit. Their look — a sleek,

TRAINER'S TIP

Bosal or Hackamore

For the first 30 days riding on a young horse, Craig often uses a rawhide bosal or hackamore, which is a braided leather noseband that works on nose and cheek pressure when the reins are applied. He finds that when horses are introduced to guiding in this manner, they learn much more quickly once they graduate to a snaffle bit. He wraps the bosal's cheeks with black electrical tape so the delicate sides of the horse's cheeks don't get rubbed by any rough rawhide.

Also, Craig likes to compete in reined cow horse events, which include hackamore classes. By using a bosal, he finds out whether or not a horse is "good in the face," meaning he guides well with nose and cheek pressure. That gives him another avenue to take the horse.

Electrical tape wrapped around the bosal helps prevent any rubbing from the braided rawhide.

single strap around a horse's head — signals that a horse is well-broke, and, therefore, they're often used in competition.

Always use a browband headstall with a snaffle bit. That setup ensures that the bridle will stay put on your horse's head. There are too many chances for a young horse to scratch his head or shake it and have a one- or split-ear headstall come off. It's fine for older horses, but not for colts just learning to carry a bit.

It's certainly acceptable to use a browband headstall with a shank bit. Cow horse riders do so all the time. That way they're sure the bridle will still be on when they charge down the fence to turn a cow.

Cavesson or Noseband

A cavesson or noseband consists of a thin headstall (or hanger) and a nosepiece (either leather or rubber) that encircles the bridge of the horse's nose. It's used to help prevent a horse from opening his mouth, especially in any response to rein pressure, thus curbing a bad habit before it becomes one.

Don't fit the cavesson too tightly. The same two-finger width you use to adjust curb chains and throatlatches applies here, as well. The idea

is to discourage opening the mouth, so that when the horse makes an attempt to do so, he runs into the noseband. He finds that he can release the pressure on himself by shutting his mouth. However, realize that if a horse wants to gap, no cavesson will keep his mouth closed.

Reins

Reins come in two basic types — split (two separate straps) and romal (one continuous loop).

Split reins are the reins of choice for most reining activities. They're two lengths of leather, typically about 7 feet long, that come in varying widths. Reiners generally prefer $5/8$-inch reins for riding trained horses and for competition. They show off a more polished horse.

With snaffles, some riders like to use a wider rein than with shank bits. The extra surface and heavier weight of the wider reins allow a young horse to feel the rein pressure better.

Romal reins are one continuous loop coupled with a romal or long strap that can be used as a quirt. They're a great tool to use when checking on how well a horse guides — running circles, changing leads, etc. When a horse isn't truly between the bridle reins, it really shows. He'll lean to one side or the other, which is obvious when you look at the reins. Also, for the rider, there's no way to cheat and pull on an inside or outside rein to steer your horse, as you can do with split reins. Your hand is wrapped around the romal, and you can't use your fingers to manipulate the reins. Therefore, you're truly riding one-handed. You can use romals four or five days in a row, then go back to split reins. Horses always seem to steer better after a time in the romals.

Martingales

Martingales are a very useful form of training equipment. They help prevent a horse from carrying his head high and are effective in teaching a horse where to position his head and neck.

The two types of martingales generally used for training reiners are running and German. (We don't discuss the third type — standing martingale — because it's too stationary and therefore restrictive for our purposes. Often called tie-downs, they have their place and are frequently used on rodeo horses and jumpers.)

A running martingale is a leather strap that runs between the horse's front legs and attaches to the cinch. It divides into two branches at the base of the horse's neck

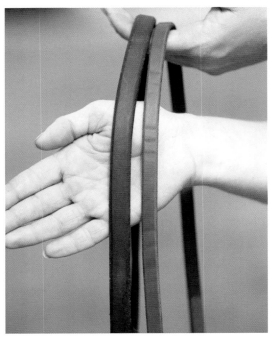

Reins comes in varying widths. Wider widths are used for training purposes and thinner ones for show.

This bit wall shows the many choices in bridle combinations, but the reiners' favorite bit is typically the correctional.

and each strap has a ring at the end through which the reins run. Some running martingales attach to the center ring of a breast collar and other outfits have a leather strap that encircles the horse's neck. Either way, the branches fork or form a "Y," stabilizing the martingale at the base of the neck.

Adjusted properly, the rings don't come up any higher than the horse's withers when the reins are picked up. The martingale shouldn't put any pressure on the horse's mouth, except when the horse raises his head too high. Adjusted too low, the rings produce a pulley effect on the horse's mouth, forcing the head down in an unnatural position.

A German martingale also consists of two leather straps that go between the horse's front legs and attach to a cinch ring. One strap runs through the left snaffle bit ring and connects to the left rein and the other runs through the right bit ring and connects to the right rein. There are three rings spaced on the German martingale reins so you can adjust the martingale pressure, depending on the length of the horse's neck.

A martingale is a good training tool, especially for 2-year-olds, because it helps teach them where to carry their heads. Although it's not meant to be used as a head-setting device, when the horse raises his head high and finds no relief, he usually lowers it.

Saddles

Saddles are a personal preference. There are many fine custom and production reining saddles on the market, so there are lots to choose from. But in general, you need a close contact seat, where you don't have a lot of leather rigging between your legs and the horse's barrel. You want to be able to feel your horse, and you want him to feel your cues.

Rigging is what connects the cinch to the saddle, and there are various positions for it depending on where it attaches to the saddletree. The range goes from full, which is positioned at the front of the saddle, to centerfire, almost under the rider's leg. For reining saddles, three-quarter rigging (midway) is a good choice, as it secures the saddle to the horse's back, yet doesn't interfere with your leg cues.

Most reining saddles have built-up pommel swells to give you something to rest your thighs against, especially in hard stops and turns. Also, the fenders can be notched (indented) for secure leg position.

The seats are often padded for extra comfort and are covered with rough-out leather to help keep you in place during the hard and fast maneuvers, especially if you're wearing rough-out chaps.

The horn should be relatively small and short. Reining saddles aren't used for roping or cutting, so you don't need tall horns to hold onto, such as in cutting, nor do you need a stout post horn to dally your rope around.

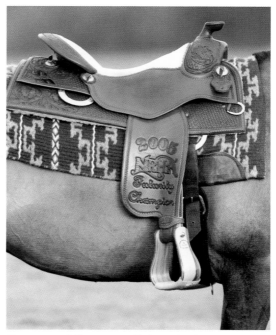

Reining saddles generally have built-up pommels, small horns and notched (indented) stirrup fenders.

Most reining saddles offer close contact, meaning there's not a lot of rigging between you and your horse.

TRAINER'S TIP

Cinch Preferences

While Craig likes to use neoprene cinches for everyday training, he prefers fleece cinches for show purposes. According to him, they look much nicer and more professional under a show saddle than neoprene.

Shawn uses neoprene cinches for both training and competition.

Fleece (left) and neoprene cinches are often the choice for both show and training.

Wool fleece pads offer lots of protection along with a great look for the show ring.

Back cinches are rarely used on reiners. There's always the chance that if you don't adjust it properly (i.e. short enough), a horse can get a hind foot shoved up in one during a hard stop.

Cinches

Because of the large number of horses in their barns, trainers generally use neoprene cinches for everyday riding because they're easy to rinse off and, therefore, help eliminate fungus or other skin conditions that can spread from horse to horse.

String cinches that are made of mohair fleece or a blend of mohair and other fibers are more breathable, which neoprene isn't. On the negative side, they're hard to dry out and keep clean, rendering them impractical in a training barn situation. However, if you have just a couple of horses and you prefer this type of cinch, then by all means use it. One advantage a string cinch has over neoprene is that it has a little bit of give to it, making it comfortable for the horse as he breaths and works hard.

Look for stainless steel fittings on any cinch you use. They don't rust and they won't break. Your life rides on the quality of gear you use, so ride the best.

When you adjust your cinch on the billet straps, make sure it's centered under your horse. Don't have one side ride higher than the other.

Saddle Pads

Navajo blanket-covered pads underlined with wool fleece are the favorite with reiners. While they aren't true Navajo blankets made by the Native American tribe famous for weaving them, they're an excellent mass-manufactured representation. They offer lots of protection and shock absorption, plus they wick moisture and look great in the show pen.

It's usually not necessary to wear two pads. That can put too much bulk between your legs and the horse and often make your saddle not fit correctly.

To prevent fungus problems, use a rubber-bottomed pad, in addition to the fleece pad, which can be easily washed off after every use.

For round-backed or mutton-withered horses, the rubber pad or a leather-bottomed pad helps keep the saddle in place as you mount and dismount and during hard maneuvers, such as spins and stops.

Protective Leg Gear

Protective leg gear is an absolute must on a reining horse. The maneuvers are too physical and the chances for injury to unprotected legs too great to ignore this important piece of equipment.

To keep your horse from hitting himself or tearing off shoes, put protective gear on him every time you ride him. The only exception might be during the early stages of riding a 2-year-old. However, when a young

A knee boot, splint boots and bell boots protect this horse's legs during a workout.

Skid boots help prevent soring a horse's fetlocks during sliding stops.

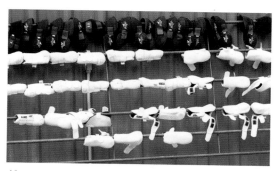

Keep your protective leg gear clean by washing them after every time you ride.

horse starts turning around or stopping, it needs some protection.

In general, the rule is to use splint or sports medicine boots, along with bell boots, on the horse's front legs and, when you practice stopping, skid boots on hind legs.

Polo wraps can be used all the way around. They're preferred by many English riders and racehorse trainers, but western riders use them, too. They're made of felt or cotton material, usually about 3 inches wide.

Knowing how to wrap a horse's leg properly is crucial because if you do it wrong (too tight), you could cause serious injury to the horse's ligaments and tendons. Have someone knowledgeable show you how to wrap, and even how to put on any protective leg gear correctly. Boots are a little more forgiving, but you can still adjust them too tightly, and they shouldn't be left on too long. They can generate a lot of heat and cause the tendons to swell. Remove them immediately after you're done riding.

Boots are usually made of leather and/or synthetic materials and fasten with buckles or Velcro®. They're easier to get on than polo wraps and offer more protection and support.

Splint or sports medicine boots protect the horse's splint and cannon bones. Bell boots cover the horse's coronary bands and heel bulbs. Some combination boots cover the entire leg from below the knee to the hoof. Skid boots protect the horse's hind fetlocks from burning when a horse stops hard.

For a horse that's particularly physical when he stops, you might put polo wraps on his hind legs and the skid boots over them.

During a practice, immediately after you're done stopping, take the skid boots off. Wearing them too long, especially the leather variety, can rub a horse and make him sore enough to stop stopping.

You might consider putting knee boots on a horse that has trouble turning and hits his knees a lot. Alternate the days – put one on the right knee one day and on the left the next. You don't want the horse to become too dependent on one side, so switch out. Wearing both is a little bulky, so use one at a time.

Whatever boots you use, keep them clean every day. Don't ride with dirt-encrusted boots or you'll risk soring your horse.

Keeping tack and equipment clean is the mark of a true horseman. Some saddle soap and leather conditioner are needed to maintain your gear in good working order. High-use items, such as boots, pads and cinches, last longer with care and quality leather goods will last a lifetime.

6

OUR APPROACH TO TRAINING

While there are no "hard and fast" rules to training reining horses, there are philosophical approaches and proven methods that have stood the test of time.

In this chapter, we'll offer some well-founded guidelines for your training program, whether it's geared toward competing in high-dollar aged events or simply reining classes in general. They consist of the philosophies and strategies that have worked well for us in our training and showing experience, no matter if we're working with 2-year-olds or older horses.

We dig into the "how-to" specifics of the foundation basics and individual maneuvers in subsequent chapters, but here are a few good thoughts to train by.

Typical Training Program

The traditional time to start a 2-year-old reining horse is between January and April, depending on the mental and physical maturity of the horse. A youngster shouldn't be ridden hard or long, maybe 30 minutes at a time. His attention span isn't long; it's much like that of a child's. There's only so much to work with at one time, so don't overdo your training sessions. Keep them short.

During a training session, if you find a colt that does everything you ask in the first 15 minutes, you might actually get off for the day and put him away. There's no reason to grind a young horse into the ground. Sometimes you can get carried away with riding a good one. They just give you so much; but be careful or you might cause one to become an underachiever instead of an overachiever. A young horse can't take much mental or physical pressure, so go easy.

It's critical to be very consistent with your hands, legs and voice — with everything you do. Your routine must be exact day in and day out or your horse will become confused, then angry and resentful. You'll have a problem on your hands that might not be easy to fix if it can be fixed at all.

Suppling your horse should be the first thing you do before asking for any maneuvers, so work on getting the resistance out of a horse's chin (mouth) and neck every day. (Suppling exercises are in the chapter titled "A Solid Foundation.") Some days that's all you'll do. It's a daily maintenance issue from the time a horse is 2 years old and upward. Your horse must understand that he has to submit and be supple.

Work on elementary reining maneuvers for at least six months or so to solidify the cues. For a horse to really understand something, he must do it about 100

Well-groomed and well-fed, the horse is ready to be well-trained.

times. So practice the maneuvers perfectly every day until you have done them at least 100 times total (over time) before you add speed or change anything in your program. Stick to slow and easy and 100 times and you'll get farther faster than if you ram and jam and try to get it all in the first six months.

Keep your horse happy in his job. Cranking on him every day isn't the answer. You want your horse fresh coming out of his 2-year-old year so that by January of his 3-year-old year he's performing all of the rudimentary reining maneuvers and is ready to advance.

Typically, your daily program for a 3-year-old should consist of all the reining maneuvers.

(Each maneuver has its own chapter.) How deep you get into them depends on how your horse is that day. If he's progressing and getting more confident, then leave him alone. If he needs a little bit of help, work on that area.

Circling and guiding are crucial every day. If the steering mechanism isn't there, nothing else will matter, so make sure your guidance systems are in place. By the time he's 3, your horse should give willingly to rein pressure by breaking or flexing at the poll. Work on getting the horse into the correct frame and performing the maneuvers in cadence. Slow and correct will someday lead to fast and correct.

Also, never have a young horse associate training with any soreness. If your horse is

A 2-year-old shouldn't be ridden hard or long.

Be consistent with how and when you cue with your hands. They're probably your most important means of communication.

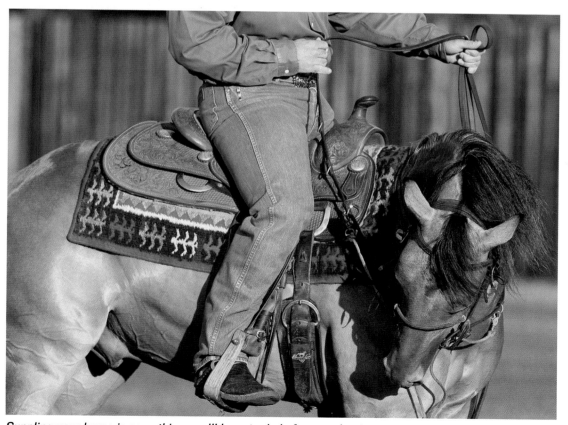

Suppling your horse is something you'll have to do before you begin any training session.

"off" somewhere or just doesn't feel well, check into it with your veterinarian and give your horse the time he needs to heal.

Overtraining

In training, maxing out (asking for a maximum effort) your horse in his maneuvers every day will burn him out for sure. He'll get mentally and physically tired of answering the same question that hard every day. He'll begin to resent his job. He'll start swishing his tail and pinning his ears, and you won't get a willing performance out of him. Also, most injuries occur when there's too much pressure day in and day out.

Ask for the basics often in warming up the horse, but for a hard stop or fast spin, the kind you'd compete with, ask only once or twice a week. You can lope him to a stop or slowly turn him, but back off for a while if he's progressing nicely and knows his job. You can even give him a weeklong vacation from hard training. Keep him legged up and in condition, but give him a rest from maneuvers. Then, after the break, ask him hard (after a sufficient warm-up) and see what he's got.

Circling and guiding are crucial exercises. If the steering mechanism isn't there, nothing else matters.

Also, speed isn't necessary every day. If you ask for it too often, before long, you'll have used up all the "try" a horse has in him, and he won't have any left for show day.

Work Ethic and Time Off

Working a horse an hour one day and five minutes the next doesn't send a good message to the horse. Some horses have good work ethics and some don't. As a rider, trainer and horseman, it's your job to encourage your horse to realize that he's got a job to do, a career. You can do that by working him consistently every day or at least giving him the same amount of work when you do train him.

However, time off, strategically planned, is a good thing. Ride the horse five days a week if he's good, six if he needs work. Give him a day or two off, however, to give him a well-deserved break. Training taxes any horse's body.

We often find horses are so much better after having a short break from training. Sometimes we give them a week off. It always seems that they come back stronger.

Also, give your horse some play time. He needs it. Don't expect him to come out of the stall on Monday the way you put him up on a Friday. He might need to blow off some steam, so give him time to do it.

As often as you can, turn your horse out to let him relax. It's tough when horses have to stay in stalls 24/7. It's not good for their minds or bodies. So if at all possible, give your horse a little R&R in between training sessions.

Knowing When to Quit

When you're training a horse (or even simply riding one), use common sense. If a horse is blowing hard through his nostrils, allow him to cool off. Stand under a shade tree, rinse off his legs, whatever, but cool him down.

There's a fine line between asking a horse to do his job hard and knowing when he's had enough. A true horseman knows when to quit.

You're dealing with an animal bred to have the desire to perform — almost like a Border Collie, who's bred to work livestock. No matter how tired he is or how hot it is, a good stock dog keeps going until he completely collapses. As a horseman, you need to step in and realize that the horse needs a break.

When the horse is out of air and you keep working him, you're asking for disaster. If the horse's air supply depletes, that means he's not getting enough oxygen to his muscles, tendons and ligaments. When they're deprived of oxygen, the fibers stretch and sometimes tear, causing an injury.

If your horse performs a particularly good stop or spin, you just might reward him by getting off and putting him away for the day. No sense in pushing him farther to get more and risk injuries.

A horse needs a physical and mental break from training. Time spent in a paddock or pasture can do a world of good for the horse's mind and body.

Give your horse breaks during training sessions. He needs time to catch his breath between exercises and maneuvers.

Also, if your horse doesn't feel right all of a sudden — he might not be visibly lame, but he's stopping wrong after stopping strong all year — then have the vet check him out.

Anger Management

If you become angry and frustrated during a training session, and you will, just get off and separate yourself from the problem. Go to lunch or do something else while you try to figure out what's going wrong. That's better than getting into a battle with a 1,000-pound animal. When you're in the middle of a storm, you find yourself reacting to what the horse is doing. You don't have time to analyze things because they happen so fast. When you reflect on the situation later, it might dawn on you what the horse was trying to do. The answer to your problem will come much faster than if you tried to "work it out" while you're upset.

Peaking Too Early

Remember that young horses in training learn something new every day. They're like

sponges in what they soak in and retain. How much and how fast they learn is partly up to them as individuals and the rest is up to you as the trainer.

If your horse is destined for the "big futurity" (NRHA Futurity) in December, then you don't want to have him peaked too early, say spring or early summer. That leaves too much time for things to happen. Your horse could fall apart, mentally or physically, and you'll have to put him back together again.

Try to have your horse ready to show one-handed by midsummer to early fall, so your horse is solid by futurity time. This doesn't mean peaked to where you're running full tilt and your horse can handle the pressure. You want him soft and solid in his maneuvers, one-handed, but leave some "gas in the tank" for the big fall futurities. Don't run the wheels off your horse in early summer and then expect to have a horse left by fall.

During the early shows, if you know your horse has an easy time with a maneuver, say he can plus half (score a half point) a stop or turnaround, then show him to his potential, if it doesn't rattle him to do so. But if he's still struggling to 0 a maneuver and you try to plus 1 it, that will come back to haunt you later down the road at a bigger and more important event. Just show what you've got in the early shows and don't go for the gusto so soon.

From the early shows in the summer you'll have around four months to improve any sticky areas that your horse has. The early shows will point out what you need to work on.

Is Your Horse Ready?

As your horse becomes more dependable in his training and you're contemplating showing him, you might try bringing him out of his stall and with minimal warm-up, ask him for a maneuver, such as a large fast circle, spin or stop. See how he handles it. If he's good, then he's ready to show and shouldn't need much more hard tuning up on a daily basis. But if he's a little ratty, then it's time to continue the drills until the horse is solid on his maneuvers without you having to demand that he be good.

The goal is to have a horse that doesn't need a lot of warm-up. There might be times when you won't have any. Sometimes, things happen at a show to prevent you from having sufficient time to warm up your horse before a class. It's good to know you don't need an hour to tune your horse. You can be ready in 10 minutes. If your horse does need an hour or more, then perhaps he's not ready to show. You'd better go back to the drawing board.

Training should be done at home. There's no sense taking your horse to the show if you're still training him in his maneuvers. You'll accomplish nothing but a bad experience for both you and your horse.

The horse show should be reserved for "tweaking" only. It's not the place to get into any major discussions with your horse. If you do, go back home and talk about it there.

Setting Goals

One of the objectives of a good training program is to be able to set goals for yourself and your horse. Make some that are definitely reachable with your and your horse's level of expertise. Then set some that are a bit higher and one big one that will take a considerable effort on your part to accomplish. For example, your first goal might be to just get through a pattern at a local schooling show. Your second set of goals might be to compete in an NRHA-sanctioned show or qualify for the NRHA affiliate finals from your region. The "big" one might be to feel confident enough to some day show at one of the NRHA aged events, such as the Futurity or Derby, or the National Reining Breeders Classic.

If you set good goals, keep in mind that there's nothing you can't do. You just have to work hard at it. But realize that it might not happen all in one year. It might take three, four or even five years to accomplish all your goals, much less your "big" one.

Riding large fast circles one-handed and on a loose rein is a good test to see if you're ready to compete.

First, set competition goals you can easily achieve, then some that will take a great effort on your part.

7

A SOLID FOUNDATION

A ll well-broke horses have good foundations, and reining horses are the epitome of well-broke horses. By foundation we mean the basic training a horse undergoes in the early stages of being ridden under saddle. During that time a horse learns to walk, trot, lope, turn, stop, back and guide on command and be responsive to hand, leg and even vocal cues.

In this book, it's not our intention to start from "day one" and show you how to accomplish the first ride on a green colt or filly. There are plenty of excellent books on the subject of starting horses under saddle.

For the purposes of this book, we'll concentrate on progressing with an already started 2-year-old. We assume that he's had

Reining is the basics of training refined to the ultimate, but a horse must learn to walk before he can run.

plenty of ground handling and is comfortable with being saddled and bridled.

Most of what we do is quite similar to what trainers in other disciplines do to accustom their young horses to under-saddle training. However, our techniques focus on developing an animal that's extremely light and responsive to rein and leg cues; in other words, a reining horse. Realize, though, that everything we talk about as far as foundation training is

Herd hierarchy is strong. All the boss broodmare has to do is bat her ears and subordinate horses scatter.

also applicable to older horses that could no doubt benefit from a refresher course.

Here's a rundown of the basics we instill in each horse before we begin training for reining maneuvers.

Pressure and Release

In training any horse, there's one thing you must remember: A horse understands where the pressure is not. That's a simple statement, but it packs a wallop and is central to our entire training program. We'll explain.

All horses understand pressure and yielding to pressure. It's inherent in their nature. They evolved as herd animals over millions of years. As herd creatures, horses innately know how to follow a leader and take direction from the leader. In their society, there's a hierarchy starting with the most dominant horse (the leader) to the second most dominant horse all the way down to the most submissive. Each horse knows its place in the herd.

Watch horses in a herd situation or actually any two horses that come into contact with one another. The dominant horse will bat his ears and make a nasty face at the subordinate horse, which immediately backs

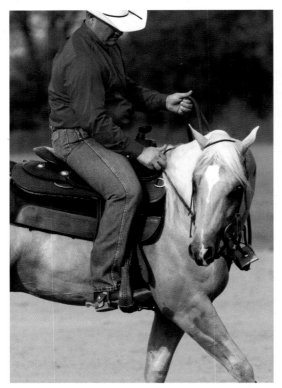

The young horse responds to right rein pressure by giving his head to the right.

Instant release is the horse's reward and how he learns what's expected of him. Remember the axiom: The horse understands where the pressure is not.

away. The dominant horse just placed pressure on the submissive one, and the latter knew the consequences of not yielding to that pressure promptly. If he didn't comply, a good, swift kick from the dominant horse would reinforce his command to move out of the way. What does that mean to you in your training program? The answer: Working with, not against, a horse's herd mentality produces the best and fastest results.

Therefore, your job is to be the dominant leader in your herd of two. As the leader, you ask certain things of your horse in a consistent manner. That's the pressure. When your horse complies with your request, you immediately stop asking. That's the release. The faster you reward with a release, the faster the horse will understand that he answered the question correctly.

All a horse wants to do is find relief from the pressure your commands place upon him. For example, if you tug on a rein, he wants to find the answer to your question so you'll stop tugging. He might turn or stop, move his head up or down, but he'll keep trying until he figures out what you want. When he does, he'll remember and do it again when you apply the same pressure.

The same goes for leg pressure. If you lay your leg against his rib cage, your horse soon learns to move away from that feeling.

Understanding what you want from him creates an "a-ha" moment for your horse, as if a light bulb goes off in his head. He remembers to repeat that response the next time around.

All of our training methods revolve around this simple concept of pressure and the release of pressure. Actually, it's at the heart of any successful training program. In ours, we aim to keep things simple from the beginning. In a nutshell: We apply consistent pressure and offer quick release. You'd be surprised how keeping things simple in the beginning helps create incredibly intricate and complicated maneuvers in the future.

In this chapter, we'll explain how pressure and release affect the elements of steering, stopping, backing, turning and rolling back – all which will one day turn into high-level reining maneuvers.

The Round Pen

Generally, horses are taught the basics in a round pen because it's a small area where they can focus on the lessons at hand.

However, staying in the round pen too long has its drawbacks. For example, it can possibly teach a horse to lean into a circle because he's constantly circling in the pen's small diameter. When a horse leans, he drops his shoulder in that direction. To perform the

The first classroom for most young horses is the round pen.

For the basic suppling exercise, pull one rein toward your hip to bring the horse's head around. The colt might start walking in a tight circle.

In this photo, the left rein is the direct rein and the right the indirect or supporting rein, which one day turns into the neck-rein.

reining maneuvers correctly, a horse must keep his shoulders up and straight. Dropping them is a bad habit to cultivate. As soon as control of the horse is established, advance to a larger arena. But, in the beginning it's easier for the horse to concentrate when he's in a small space.

Basic Suppling Exercise

The first thing you must work on with any horse is suppleness. Your horse must be flexible through his head and neck before he can steer or guide well.

To supple your horse, put him in a smooth snaffle bit (see the "Tack and Equipment" chapter). Horses are typically started in snaffle bits because they have mild mouthpieces and provide the lateral pull needed in suppling exercises.

Gently pull one rein toward your hip, bringing the horse's head around. Your horse will probably walk in a tight circle, but keep holding until he stops moving his feet. When he does, release your hold. That tells him you

want him to give his head, not move his feet. Suppling a horse's head and neck is usually the first lesson in pressure and release.

In the beginning, hold for only a couple of seconds, but work up to longer periods of time in which your horse gives his head willingly. Do both sides equally.

This basic suppling exercise should start all your training sessions, whether they're with a green colt or a seasoned competitor. You can never supple a horse enough and most all horses need to be reminded of it throughout their entire riding careers.

The Guiding Principle

The defining aspect of reining is to be able to guide the horse. Guiding, or teaching your horse to steer, starts in a round pen with two reins attached to a simple snaffle bit. One rein is called the direct rein because it has a direct pull on the horse's mouth and influences the horse to move in the direction of the pull. When you pull right, the horse follows right. When you pull left, the horse follows left.

The young horse learns where to place his head when he begins flexing at the poll.

The other rein is the indirect or supporting rein, which you lay across the horse's neck. It works indirectly on the horse's mouth, thus the name, and eventually develops into the neck-rein when you ride one-handed later on in your horse's training.

Which rein is which depends on the direction you're traveling. For example, start at a walk and ask your horse to steer to the right by gently pulling the right rein out to the side and laying the left rein on the horse's neck to support the direct rein. Use only enough pressure to see the outside of the horse's right eye. (The idea here is to turn your horse, not supple your horse's neck, as in the basic suppling exercise.) The direct rein leads the horse to the right, and the indirect rein reinforces your request. The instant your horse yields to the rein and takes a step to the right, release all pressure. Repeat the procedure until your horse responds consistently to the rein pressure.

To steer left, pull the left rein out to the side and reinforce it by laying the right rein on the horse's neck. Release your pressure the second your horse takes a step to the left.

Eventually, you'll need only the neck-rein to guide your horse, but for now help him out with both reins.

The direct and indirect reins are also called the inside and outside reins, depending again on the direction you're going. If moving or circling to the right, the inside rein would be your right rein and the outside rein the left one. Vice versa for traveling to the left.

These same distinctions apply to your legs, as well. Your inside leg is the one to the inside of the circle. For example, in circling to the right, your right leg is the inside leg and your left is the outside leg.

We're jumping a bit ahead of ourselves here, but as you progress in your practice in the months to come, you'll start using the neck-rein first, then follow with the direct rein as needed. In time, your horse will learn to pay attention to the neck-rein, and you won't need the direct rein. The sequence is "outside rein – inside rein," which means use the outside (neck) rein first, and, if the horse doesn't respond, follow with the direct rein.

A Head Start

At the same time you work on guiding, you can introduce the concept of head placement. Don't expect immediate and consistent vertical flexion from a green 2-year-old, but certainly you can begin to develop the elements of a headset with softness and suppleness in the horse's poll. The goal is to have your horse give to bit pressure by flexing at his poll when he feels you pick up on the reins. We also refer to this as "giving in the face," being "soft in the face," "bridling up" or "being in the bridle."

With your horse still in a simple snaffle, walk him around the pen. Squeeze your legs and drive your horse up into the bit. Hold your reins still and taut. Your horse will feel the wall of bit pressure and it'll be uncomfortable. He'll struggle at first and try to evade the pressure in various ways — raising his head, turning it to the side, opening his mouth, pushing against the bit, etc. The second he gives his head (bends at the poll), release your reins. This might take 15 to 20 strides or more on a green horse, but you're teaching him that when he breaks at the poll, he'll find relief. You might have to do this many times a day for many months before the horse responds with any consistency.

After success at a walk, move into a jog. Drive your horse forward into the bit and wait for him to drop his head. When he does, release instantly. Again, it's pressure and release, as in everything else you do. Once your horse responds well at the lower gaits, moving into the lope is no problem.

Steer your horse all over the pen, in straight lines and circles, asking him to give to the bridle through rein pressure and bit pressure. Reward him every time he moves off the rein and gives to the bit. You'll have to work on these two things every day before you can go on to other maneuvers. There might be days when it's all you do. That's okay. Your horse must understand that he's got to be supple and submit to the pressure. It's central to your entire reining training program.

When there's little or no resistance in the neck, face and chin, you're on the right road to neck-reining and a proper head-set.

Move Off Your Leg

You've worked on getting your horse to move off rein and bit pressure, now introduce leg pressure. A good way to get your horse to move off your leg is to teach him to side-pass, a lateral movement. In this maneuver, the horse's body moves sideways, with one set of legs crossing over the other.

To start, position your horse's body with his head facing the round pen fence, which puts him perpendicular to it. The fence acts as a barrier, keeping your horse from moving forward. Take hold of both reins to steady the horse and keep him straight with the fence. That prevents him from moving his head to the right or left.

To side-pass to the right, bump your horse's left rib cage with your left leg (or apply steady left leg pressure, whichever cue seems to work best for your horse). Take your right leg off his side, in effect opening up a doorway. The

For a side-pass, you might have to exaggerate your body position in the beginning. Here, to move to the left, place your right leg on the horse's side and open up your left leg. Steady the horse's front end with reins in both hands.

When introducing the word "whoa" to a young horse, let the round pen fence stop him.

second he takes one step to the right, stop bumping or pressing. To side-pass to the left, bump or apply pressure with your right leg, remove any left leg pressure and, again, as soon as he makes a step (to the left), stop bumping or release and let him rest.

Be happy with one step at a time, then two, then three. It might take awhile for your horse to make the connection. Also, most horses are better one way than the other.

No doubt, in the beginning, your horse will look for avenues to escape the pressure. He might lean into the pressure, instead of moving off it. He might toss his head up, down or to the right or left. He might even back. Keep his body straight between the reins and use leg pressure if he backs instead of moves sideways.

Work both directions equally. As in anything, whatever you do on one side, do likewise on the other. You want your horse to be balanced on both sides of his brain. Horses have a right and left half to their brains and each must be taught independently. Just because he can do something to the right doesn't mean he understands how to do it to the left.

Just Say "Whoa"

You've probably heard or seen the phrase, "Just say 'whoa.'" It's a catchy slogan you'll see a lot on T-shirts, coffee mugs, you name it. However, in our stopping program, we do more than just say "whoa." Actually, we like to have three brake controls — hand, voice and feet. You can pull back on the reins, say "whoa" and/or shove your feet forward in the stirrups. Having all three controls allows you to stop the horse off one, two or all three cues. This comes in handy someday when you show the horse. If the horse forgets what one cue means, you still have two more to fall back on.

Introduce the stop in a round pen, using the fence as a barrier, much as you'll do in a big arena when you fence your horse. Walk toward the fence, bumping or squeezing with your legs to keep him moving forward. Say "whoa" when he comes up to the fence, pull back on the reins and push your feet out front. When he comes to a complete stop, release your rein hold and bring your feet back. Since the fence stops the horse's forward motion, the horse generally makes a quick connection with the stopping cues.

However, later, out in the large arena, your horse might keep trucking instead of stopping. If and when this occurs, lift your hands

If, out in a larger arena, the colt doesn't respond to the "magic word," lift the reins to create more of an uncomfortable barrier with the bit.

After stopping, back a few steps. If your horse gets sticky, flutter your legs alongside the horse's shoulders.

TEACH THE TURNAROUND

1. In this right turnaround sequence, the horse was trotting to the left. The outside or right rein turns the horse into the fence. The lack of space encourages the horse to use his hindquarters for turning.

2. The horse's left front leg crosses over the right.

3. The cross-over is complete.

4. The right front leg moves over.

5. The left front leg crosses over again in the continuation of the turnaround.

6. The right front leg moves to the right.

In our program, "whoa" means stop and back up. Therefore, after you stop, back a few steps. To encourage your horse to back, flutter or slap your legs on his shoulders. Your horse will look for a way out and when he takes a step back, release your legs and drop your rein hands on the mane.

If your horse backs crooked, use your leg to slap the horse's shoulder on the side he's crooked. That blocks his movement. If he refuses to back, don't release the reins until he gives you one step backward. Then reward by giving him slack. Don't ask him to back 20 or 30 steps in the beginning. Young or inexperienced horses, especially, won't understand backing that far.

You might have to stop and back your horse this way 20 or 30 times a day for 30 days. That's what it takes to make something sink in to your horse. Remember that a horse has to do something at least 100 times before he can retain it. He'll come to associate the word "whoa" with stopping and backing. When you lay your hands down, it's the signal to stop altogether.

After your horse has mastered the stop and back-up from a walk, tip him up into the trot and repeat the same procedure trotting into the round pen fence, then in the arena.

7. The horse has almost made one full revolution to the right and is facing left again. Notice how his hind feet have remained relatively stationary.

a little and hold steady pressure until he comes to a stop. By lifting your hands, you make the bit contact more uncomfortable for him. Eventually he figures out that ceasing forward motion gives him some slack and therefore reward.

For a snappy rollback, ask the horse for speed by smooching or clucking.

The young horse learns to power out of the rollback.

In the early stages of teaching your horse to stop, stopping from a trot isn't as much of a shock on his hocks as it is at a lope. Your horse probably won't have slide plates on his hind feet at this time, so don't expect him to slide at all. He's doing good just to stop his forward motion on command and take a few steps backward.

When you're confident he can stop from a trot, try it at a lope. Don't be surprised if the first time your horse flips his head around and comes up out of the ground. That's normal. Don't punish him for stopping poorly in the beginning. Just keep it up until he starts using his hind legs as brakes.

If your horse pulls a little one way or the other, wait until you get stopped and back before you pull him in the opposite direction as a correction. Don't make a big deal out of it early on, just enough to let him know he did wrong.

This might be all you should do for the first six months of training. Nothing fast, just at a slow lope. After six months, ask for more speed to see if he can handle it.

It's really easy to burn up a good, young horse. One that shows a lot of try and promise at an early age makes it tempting to want to do more with him. But restrain yourself. Two-year-olds, especially, need time to mature, mentally and physically. They can start resenting their jobs in a hurry if you rush them.

Rollback and Turnaround

Cues for starting the horse on rollbacks (180-degree turns) and turnarounds (360-degree turns) in the round pen are similar, with the turnaround being built off the rollback.

Use the round pen fence as part of the exercise. It acts as a barrier through which the horse can't go. He learns to use his hindquarters as he turns, which is the objective in both rollbacks and turnarounds.

For the beginnings of a rollback, trot your horse in small circles next to the fence. After a few circles, pull the outside rein as you ride next to the fence. This encourages the horse to shift his weight onto his hindquarters, as there's little room for turning when you're next to the fence. Also, the fence helps pull

As the horse develops self carriage, he begins to carry himself in a collected frame. Note the level top line on this 2-year-old colt. Also, he flexes nicely at the poll, already exhibiting signs of collection, and all on a loose rein.

the horse through the turn, so you don't have to use your reins the entire time. It allows you to leave the horse's face alone during the turning maneuver, which is your aim in all the maneuvers.

For example, to roll back to the right, trot small left circles close to the fence. After a couple, take your right rein as you pass alongside the fence and ask your horse to turn into the fence. The second he turns, release your rein. He should step across, his left leg over his right leg. You'll have turned 180 degrees to face the opposite direction, and that's a rollback.

Encourage your horse to push out of a rollback at the lope by clucking or smooching or even tapping him on the rump with the reins if need be. The idea is to push out of there with strong forward motion.

To roll back the opposite direction, bring him back down to the trot and make a couple of right circles. (You can work on this exercise at the lope in the round pen; however, in the beginning go slowly and trot to get your horse's front leg cross-over correct before you add speed.) Reverse the procedure. As you circle close to the fence, take hold of your left rein and ask your horse to turn to the left by pulling his face into the fence. The instant he does, release your rein pressure, and he'll follow through on his own.

For the beginning elements of a turn-around, use the same exercise, but instead of ending with a 180-degree turn in the opposite direction, ask your horse to continue turning and complete a 360-degree turn. You should then be facing the direction you started.

After a few single 360-degree turns, make one and one half turns (a 360-degree turn followed by a 180-degree turn), which will have you facing the opposite direction. Mixing it up like this keeps your horse guessing and encourages a light response to your rein signals.

There will be times, especially in the beginning, when your horse will be stiff in his neck as you turn him into the fence. Just hold your rein steady until he gives to the pressure. Don't jerk. Any jerking or snatching at this stage of the game will only scare the horse, and he'll brace against your rein pressure, which isn't what you want.

Realize that in rolling back and turning around you're using forward motion to accomplish your goals. You're not backing into the turns, you're moving forward and turning at the same time. Forward motion is the key to executing correct rollbacks and turnarounds, and that will become really obvious as your horse progresses in his training.

The Big Pen

When you can walk, trot, lope, turn, roll back, stop and back with control in the round pen, it's time to graduate to a larger arena or slide track. Perform all the same exercises you did in the round pen to confirm in your horse's mind what riding is all about. You can ask for them next to the arena fence if it helps the horse understand and make the connection.

In the big pen, spend a lot of time just simply loping your horse quietly and softly. Loping is, after all, the main gait at which reining takes place. Steer your horse in different directions to get him used to being guided all over the pen.

As you lope, keep your rein hands low; your reins should be loose with no pressure on the horse's mouth. Don't hold your reins so high that you constantly come in contact with the horse's mouth. You want your horse to learn to go on a loose rein, not on rein contact.

This also allows your horse to develop his own style. He learns "self carriage" or how to hold himself as he maneuvers around the pen. You want his body to be soft and relaxed, and loose reins offer that to your horse. Riding with a tight rein or constantly picking on the horse's face to get him to hold his head and neck in a certain frame this early on will do nothing but make him uptight and worried about what he's doing.

Leads and Lead Departures

As you circle, ask for a simple lead departure, for example, a right lead as you circle to the right and a left lead as you circle to the left. Accomplish this much the same way you did the side-pass in the round pen. Lay your outside leg against the horse's rib cage, which pushes the hip away from pressure and onto the correct lead. Take your inside leg off the horse's side to open the doorway for him to move in that direction. At the same time, you can encourage your horse to lope off by making a smooching or clucking sound.

Don't be too critical of your horse picking up the correct leads at this time. By that we mean don't punish him for not picking up the proper one. He's simply not far enough along

Ask for simple lead departures from a trot.

Move all over the arena in a quiet, relaxed lope. Every so often, break down to a trot, pick up the other lead and lope off again. Since the lope is the main reining gait, you want your horse confident in it.

for that kind of refinement. However, don't let him continue in the wrong lead either. You want him to learn to move correctly in a circle from the beginning. Just stop and start again. For example, if you're circling to the right and he picks up the left lead, gently pull him down into the trot and start over. Be careful not to ask too abruptly with the reins. That could scare the horse because he won't know what he did wrong. Before you know it, he'll be nervous about your basic commands. So break him down from the lope slowly and carefully.

From time to time, check to make sure "someone's home" by bumping your horse with the reins and asking for his face to see if he's paying attention to you. What you're looking for is a slight give at the poll, which means the horse's jaw is relaxed enough to give to the bit.

Your horse must have all the basics down pat before you can go on with his reining training. The foundation exercises are the building blocks of high-level reining maneuvers. Miss one and it'll show up as a hole in your horse's education somewhere down the line.

"The circle is a great tattletale."

8

CIRCLES

Once you've taught your horse the basics, he's guiding well and all controls are in place, it's time for serious reining training. And while we call it serious, that doesn't mean you're going to get complicated all of a sudden. The reining maneuvers are built off the basics; they're the basics refined to their highest level, but they're still the basics.

Begin with the circle; it's the maneuver you'll work in throughout most of your training program. It's often called the foundation of reining because in a circle you can tell how well your horse is guiding. The circle is a great tattletale. It tells you whether your horse has learned his lessons. If he's between the bridle reins — not leaning one way or the other — you know your horse understands rein pressure, listens to it and respects it.

Supple and Soft

Before you begin circling, or any workout session, for that matter, always start by suppling and warming up your horse.

After you mount, check out your suppling systems. Make sure your horse is soft in the chin (giving to the bit) and neck (flexing at the poll) before you do anything else. No matter what you're doing, your horse has got to be soft in the bridle or he will not function as a true reining horse.

At the walk, go through the suppling exercises mentioned in the previous chapter, particularly those that apply to rein and leg response.

After you've suppled your horse at the walk, trot him around to warm up before starting your circling program, but at the same time, continue asking him for his face and to move off your leg. Then, move up into the lope and spend more time making sure your horse is soft in the face. You want him relaxed, quiet and in a learning mode.

Note: As you work on circles every day, you'll find yourself also working on other maneuvers, such as steering (neck-reining), lead departures, speed control, the counter-canter and lead changes. The last three we'll discuss in subsequent chapters, as they're a refinement of the basic circle.

Here are general guidelines to keep in mind, followed by some specific exercises for a comprehensive circling program.

Happy Circles

In practicing any circles, lope for as long as it takes for your horse to relax and remain quiet. If your horse is young, especially, he might wander around

A circle tells you how well your horse is guiding.

Make sure your horse is supple, gives to the bit and flexes at the poll before you begin your circling program.

with rest and/or medical attention. If he just doesn't like his job, maybe he won't make a reiner either, so watch for cues in your horse's work ethic. They'll be right in front of you. Don't ignore them.

Don't ever lope a horse to exhaustion in an effort to wear him down. The worst thing you can do to any horse is continue riding him when he's out of air. He needs a break and a breather. Break him down to a walk and let him catch his breath. Riding a horse that's overly tired is only asking for trouble. You could hurt him physically by forcing him to move on tendons and ligaments that are deprived of oxygen and therefore at risk of injury, and you could hurt him mentally by making him resent his job.

Even if you're in the middle of teaching a maneuver and trying to "make a point" to your horse, realize his physical state and back off. Give him a chance to think about it. For example, if you're introducing something new and your horse has no clue what you're asking, don't get in a hurry with him. Give him plenty of time to learn. It might take three or four weeks, even two months. So what? As long as your horse shows the desire and ability to learn, give him the time.

Perfectly Round Circle

Circles should be ridden perfectly round, not as lopsided, egg-shaped elliptical orbits. That might not be as easy as it sounds. You'll have to work at making sure your circle is round. Your horse certainly doesn't know what round is, so you'll have to guide him. Here are some little tricks to help you get the "feel" of riding true circles.

If you have an arena, the fence can supply you with reference points that you "hit" as you lope. For example, you can pick out certain posts along the fence that you use to describe the perimeter of the circle. Riding by those posts or "points" keeps you on the path of the circle.

Riding on a slide track with no fences is more of a challenge. You can put a bucket in the middle of the track and ride around it, keeping yourself equidistant from the bucket.

You can also make a visible circle, say, out on a grass pasture. Riding on the predetermined path keeps you automatically on a perfect circle. Horses are hard-wired to stay on pre-described paths and learn quickly to stay on them. In the wild, they intuitively know to follow certain trails from water hole to water

a bit at first, but steady him with the reins, bringing him back to you. If he strays off the path you're on, gently pick up the reins and put him back on track. Don't ever jerk on the reins. That only serves to scare the horse and make him nervous about them.

The idea is to keep your horse happy in his circles. Let him lope freely around the pen and watch his ears. They should be up and moving back and forth — ahead at where he's going and back listening to you. That's a good sign and means that your horse is interested in what he's doing and paying attention to you.

A horse that pins his ears flat back and wrings or swishes his tail excessively is telling you there's something wrong. He's cranky because he either hurts somewhere or is confused and therefore angry about his lessons. He can't learn in that frame of mind. Take the time to find out what's going on with your horse and correct it before it becomes a problem. If he's hurting, fix it,

When your horse needs a break, let him stop and catch his breath. Never ride a horse to exhaustion.

TRAINER'S TIP

Running Style

When you practice your circles, ask a friend or a trainer to act as another set of eyes. Have him or her watch your horse at different speeds. Every horse has a speed at which he looks best. It does no good to run the wheels off your horse if he doesn't look good doing it. It's better to stick to a medium-fast speed so the horse looks comfortable in his striding. Your other set of eyes can see it better than you can feel it, so take the observer's advice and stick to the speed that makes your horse look like a winner.

A well-guided horse stays between the bridle reins.

hole every day. The same is true of horses on a dude string. Have you ever tried to turn a dude horse? Reining horses they're not; but they do know how to stay on a trail.

Use these tips to help you perfect your circles, but the only way to really get the hang of riding them is through lots of practice. Ride circle after circle after circle, and in time they'll come naturally.

Circle Drill

Your horse's body should be in the same arc as the circle. However, this doesn't mean the horse is overly bent in either direction. His spine, from poll to tail, should remain relatively straight. Tip the horse's nose slightly to the inside of the circle. All you want to see is the horse's eyebrow, nothing more. From this position, a horse can still stop, turn and roll back.

The circle drill is an excellent exercise to help develop lightness in a horse's responses at the lope. It's a combination of circles and straight lines that teaches a horse where to put his head, and, at the same time, helps keep a horse's shoulders up and straight. Here's the drill, starting with left circles.

Pick up the left rein and tip the horse's nose to the inside. Lay your right rein (neck rein) against the right side of the horse's neck. Lope a few circles to the left. Then steer the horse out of the circle in a straight line by picking up both reins to straighten him. When he goes straight, release the reins. Lope for a few strides, then lay the right rein against the right side of the horse's neck again, pushing the horse over with a neck rein to the left. Use your direct or inside rein to tip the horse's nose to the inside. After a few more left circles, steer off in another straight line. Then repeat the sequence by guiding your horse back onto a left circle. Keep this up until the horse becomes very light and responsive to

The horse's body should be on the same arc as the circle.

The ultimate goal is to ride one-handed, at whatever maneuver or speed you're in.

For circles that catch the judge's eye, determine at which speed your horse runs best.

your slightest move. This translates nicely later when you move up to one hand on the bridle.

Tattletale

Do you remember we said that the circle is a great tattletale? It'll tattle on you if your horse isn't between the bridle reins. You can tell by simply looking at your horse's neck position. Is the neck centered between the reins or is it leaning on one of the reins? The main problem you'll have in riding circles is correcting a horse that leans to the inside. What he's doing is dropping a shoulder, causing him to duck into the center of the circle. A horse can also drop his shoulder by sticking his chin to the outside of the circle. It's a similar form of resistance as one who tips his head and neck to the center, but the fix is the same.

To fix a dropped shoulder, ride with a rein in each hand and pick up the inside rein, which, in effect, picks up the horse's shoulder. Raise it until you can feel the horse straighten and

stop leaning. Hold the outside rein steady to prevent the horse from moving to the outside of the circle. As soon as your horse straightens, put your rein back down again. Repeat as often as necessary until the horse keeps his shoulders up and straight. You can also use the circle drill as a good exercise for this problem.

However, if both of these fixes don't work to keep your horse light and straight between the reins, then, as a correction, use a sort of "reverse psychology." Break your horse down from the lope and spin him to the outside of the circle. For example, if the horse leans in a right circle, the sequence goes like this: Stop the horse's forward momentum by pulling back on the reins. Use your inside (or right) rein to pick up the dropped right shoulder and lay the rein across the right side of the horse's neck, steering him to the outside (or left). In effect, the inside rein now becomes the outside rein. At the same time, open up your outside (or left) leg as you use pressure with your inside (or right) leg to spin the horse around a couple of times to the outside of the circle (or to the left). Like the reins, your left leg, which was the outside leg, switches to become the inside leg and your inside right leg switches to become the outside leg. After a few spins to the left, continue at the lope in a left circle and see if the horse won't stay between the reins. Allow the horse to make any mistakes on his own. In this case, the second he starts to lean to the left, stop him and spin him to the right. Continue the drill until your horse stops leaning and stays between the reins.

Another way to check your horse's rein-ability is to imagine a little box in front of your saddle horn. Your goal is to keep your rein hand in that box and never leave it. Your horse should become so responsive that all you have to do is barely move your hand one way or the other and your horse follows its lead. That's what reining is all about. You lead; your horse follows. The rest of the time, your hand should rest over the middle of the horse's mane.

Lead Departures

Loping circles and teaching your horse lead departures happen at the same time. When you cue a horse to lope, you also must cue for either the right or left lead.

Although you eventually want your horse to be able to pick up his leads on a straightaway, it's easiest to introduce them while loping a circle.

Lead departures are accomplished with shoulder and hip control using rein and leg pressure. You'll move the horse's hip over to the right or left, depending on the lead. The idea is to open a doorway through which the horse can go and encourage a hind-leg-first lead departure.

In the early stages of teaching lead departures, use both reins and be at the trot. (It's easier on the horse to move into a lope from a trot than from the walk.)

To set up a right lead, lay the left rein over the left side of the horse's neck and bring the right rein out to the side, slightly higher than the left to help keep the right shoulder up. Lay your left leg on the horse's rib cage or on his flank to move his hip to the right and open up your right leg to allow the horse to go to the right. Use a smooching or clucking sound as a verbal cue to increase speed into a lope.

To pick up the left lead, reverse the procedure. Lay your right rein on the right side of the horse's neck and bring the left rein out to the side a little higher than the right. Lay your right leg on the horse's rib cage or flank and open up your left leg.

If the horse doesn't pick up the correct lead right away, don't punish him. Instead, break him back down to a trot and start over again. If you make too big a deal out of picking up leads, you'll make your horse anxious and create a problem.

Note: As time goes by, you should be able to ask for leads one-handed. Simply pick up your reins, apply leg pressure and smooch or cluck. Your horse will understand which lead to take by your leg cues, and you won't have to rein him one direction or the other. However, you might have to go back to two hands if your horse gets a little lost; that's okay. Your goal, though, is to ride one-handed because 95 percent of everything you do in your training from this point on will be with one hand.

"Speed elevates the degree of difficulty in any maneuver."

9

SPEED CONTROL

All reining patterns call for both large, fast and small, slow circles and rundowns to a stop. Controlling your horse's speed is every bit as important as the maneuvers themselves. Since you're in charge of the gas pedal, it's your job to teach your horse how to increase and decrease his speed with a system of cues. How reliable your horse is at speed is the question you have to answer. Speed always adds a degree of difficulty to anything.

In this chapter, we'll explain how to teach a horse to speed up and slow down on command and how to prevent or correct the typical problems that happen when speed is a factor.

Speed Demon

Going at speed is exciting for any horse. Some stop thinking when they start running. Since much of a reining pattern happens at speed, it's something you'll have to address throughout your training program.

A horse's personality type has a lot to do with the way he runs, and that can run the gamut. There are lazy, laid-back horses that need constant encouragement to gallop at all, and then there are hot or "juicy" horses that need no excuse to speed up. Runaways during a pattern are rare and not a pretty sight, but they do happen. Work on speed at home before you ever attempt it in a show.

Teach speed control as you would any other maneuver, through a system of cues and a lot of practice. Your horse should become as comfortable with it as anything else you do.

It's not a good idea to work on speed control with an overly fresh horse, one that has "run" on his mind. Give him a chance to learn his lessons in a quiet and settled frame of mind. Warm him up first by letting him lope freely around the arena or slide track. You can also let him run off some steam in a round pen before you ever saddle him. Once he's gotten out the kinks and is like putty in your hand, then begin the lesson.

Footfall Pattern

The speed in early speed control lessons doesn't mean blinding fast, the kind you see finished horses run in a futurity or open reining. It simply means a notch up from a slow lope to a hand gallop.

You'll achieve plenty of speed in time, so don't think you have to have it all at once. First, get the

High-scoring patterns are usually done at speed, so your horse must be as comfortable with it as he is with the maneuvers.

TRAINER'S TIP

Mix It Up

Here's a drill to help solidify speed control in your horse.

Depart on the correct lead and lope a few quiet, slow circles. When your horse shows that he's relaxed, ask for some speed. Play "horse show" a little bit and pretend you're in a large, fast circle.

Steer your horse all over the arena, mixing up the large, fast and small, slow circles to keep him guessing.

Sometimes run a full circle, sometimes a half. Then run fast for half a circle and ask your horse to come back down into a slow circle.

You'll find that your horse might lose some of his form in his large, fast circles, so practicing them in conjunction with small, slows is beneficial.

horse broke to the idea of speed and moving back and forth between a lope and gallop.

Horses actually change footfall patterns when they move from a three-beat lope to a four-beat gallop.

The lope begins with one hind leg striking the ground first, followed by the opposite hind leg and its diagonal front leg striking second. The third beat is the foreleg opposite the initial hind leg. It's called the leading leg since it reaches farther forward than the other front leg, hence the term right lead or left lead. There's a moment of suspension when all four legs are off the ground, just before the hind leg strikes the ground again. The sequence for a left lead is: right hind, left hind and right front, left front, suspension. The sequence for a right

At the beginning of a practice, lope a fresh horse freely around the track until he's totally relaxed and ready for work.

lead is: left hind, right hind and left front, right front, suspension.

In the gallop, both hind legs strike in sequential order, then the front legs in the same order, followed by a moment of suspension before the initial hind leg strikes again. The leading leg is the last front leg to strike the ground. The sequence for a left lead is: right hind, left hind, right front, left front (lead), suspension. The sequence for a right lead is: left hind, right hind, left front, right front (lead), suspension.

The Gas Pedal

Compare speed control on your horse to the gas pedal on your car. When you mash down on the pedal, your speed increases. The harder you mash, the faster you go. To slow down, you ease off the pedal.

When it comes to your horse's gas pedal, you have the luxury of using verbal cues along with physical cues, unlike in a car. The cues are simple and there are more than one for both speeding up and slowing down. Here's what we do.

To ask for an increase in speed, use leg pressure by squeezing your legs around your horse's belly. By this time, your horse has learned to move away from leg pressure and he'll scoot forward. At the same time, lean forward in the saddle (over the saddle horn). By shifting your weight forward, you get over your horse's center of gravity, located by the withers during a gallop. This helps free up your horse and allow him to run.

"Chase" your horse with your rein hand up toward your horse's ears. Chasing him (on a loose rein) is additional body language that urges him forward faster. Stretch your arm out, take the bend out of your elbow. It looks aggressive to the judge, like you're going all out and makes a really nice picture in the arena. At home, practice guiding your horse from this position so he understands the feel of the reins high on his neck.

Also, use a verbal cue, such as a clucking, kissing or smooching sound. This should become your universal cue to speed up, no matter what your horse is doing — galloping or spinning. Over time, he'll learn that you want him to hustle when he hears the sound.

To slow down, sit back down in the saddle and release your leg pressure. Your weight shift backward is an immediate signal to your horse to slow down, as is the lack of leg pressure.

TRAINER'S TIP

The Need for Speed

During your practice at home before a show, don't just lope slowly, then come the day of the show, blast your horse around the arena. He'll most likely fall apart if he's not used to the speed. Practice the speed at home that you intend to show at during the show.

It's not necessary to gallop hard and fast every day at home, but at least a few times during the week, ask for increased speed.

In addition, use a verbal cue, such as a humming sound or the word "easy." (We like to hum; it's less distracting in a horse show situation.) You can use any verbal cues you want, but find ones that suit you and be consistent with them. For example, a smooch or kissing sound always means to hurry up and a hum means to slow down.

When you speed up a horse for the first time, especially a young one, he might be erratic. He might look to the right or left and, in general, act uncomfortable. If necessary, ride with two hands to steady your horse, keep him in the correct frame and at a reasonable speed. Don't let him go full out in the beginning. Gradually ask for an increase in speed, but don't push him to go racehorse fast. He'll essentially move from a slow, three-beat lope into a four-beat gallop.

Twice as Many Slow

Start out by loping slow circles. Ask for the lead departure on a straight line. That way your horse doesn't associate picking up a lead with making an immediate circle.

Also, by loping slowly, your horse doesn't get into the habit of charging out of a lead departure, so lope at least one circle in a slow speed before you move up into faster circles.

Gallop your horse around the arena or track until you feel him relax. Your objective is to have a horse comfortable with speed, and the only way he can do that is to do it often enough that it's second nature to him. Gallop until he feels like he wants to quit. Go a few more strides, then ask him to slow down.

Always lope twice as many small, slow circles as you do large, fast to encourage your horse to think "slow." There are some patterns that ask for a small, slow circle out of a lead departure. If your horse thinks he has to gallop right away, you'll have to pull him back down and that won't look good to the judge.

SPEED CONTROL

1.

2.

3.

1., 2., and 3. Begin at a slow, three-beat lope.

4.

5.

4., 5., and 6. Build speed by leaning forward in the saddle and "chasing" your horse with the reins forward on his neck. Your horse should move into a four-beat gallop.

6.

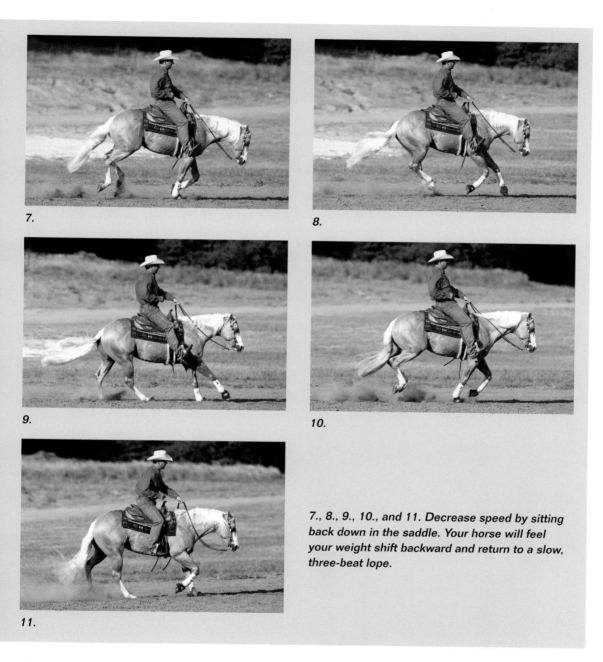

7.

8.

9.

10.

11.

7., 8., 9., 10., and 11. Decrease speed by sitting back down in the saddle. Your horse will feel your weight shift backward and return to a slow, three-beat lope.

The Center of the Pen

The center of the arena is a place where a lot of things happen — stops, spins, lead departures, etc. These can be exciting things to a horse; don't make speeding up one of them. Go a few strides past the center and then push him into the gallop. That helps prevent your horse from becoming chargey in the middle.

After a couple of large, fast circles, come through the middle and ask your horse to slow down. We like to use a humming sound because with it we don't have to use our reins to slow the horse and that presents a quieter picture to the judge. But, as mentioned earlier, you can slow your horse with whatever cue you normally use — rein pressure, release of leg pressure, body posture, the word "easy," whatever. Just be consistent.

Ease on Down

However in conjunction with your cue, keep your outside leg on your horse and take your inside leg off to move into a slower speed. There are a couple of reasons why.

If your horse doesn't respond to your cues to slow down, take hold of him and pull him into the ground, if necessary, then start over.

One, sometimes when a horse shuts down from fast to slow, he'll fall out of lead behind. The sudden decrease, often within a stride or two, causes him to have to re-balance himself from a fast four-beat gallop to a slower three-beat lope. Your outside leg serves to shove his hip to the inside, ensuring he keeps his lead by blocking his hip from moving to the outside. If he switches hips, he'll accidentally switch leads — not what you want.

Also, since in a reining pattern lead changes are performed in the center of the pen, your horse might get confused and think he must change leads once he hits the middle and switch on you. You can beat him to the punch and change his mind by keeping an outside leg on him.

Two, if you were to immediately go from a large, fast circle to a small, slow one in the middle, your horse might drop his shoulder (along with falling out of lead behind) if you don't keep his shoulders up by steering straight. You can inadvertently teach your horse to drop his shoulder that way. That's why you should slow down and move straight for a few strides. A really broke horse can speed up and slow down on a straight line, but it's hard to do. Then continue in a large slow circle, rather than transition to a small circle right away. Complete one large circle at the slower speed, followed by five or six smaller circles.

Here's a scenario to practice speed control, moving from slow to fast to slow.

Lope a normal size circle at normal speed. Continue through the middle at that speed, then increase your speed at the top of the circle by wrapping your legs around your horse's belly. You're not asking for full-out speed at this point, just an increase.

Come through the center at that speed, but hum to your horse to ask him to slow down. Take hold of him with both reins if necessary. Continue to lope the normal size circle. When you come to the center, steer into the small circle and do about a half dozen of them, with your outside leg on the horse the whole time to keep his lead from falling out behind.

The Speed Police

If your horse doesn't respond to your humming or cue to slow down, take hold of him, not overly hard, but so he knows he's being reprimanded. Pull him into the ground; then start your circle again. If he still doesn't listen, pull him down and spin him twice to the inside. Depart again.

Don't snatch at your horse's face when you take hold. That might scare him and he'll become leery of the reins and start overreacting to your commands — the last thing you want. The scare might cause his adrenaline to flow and the next time he comes through the middle, he might speed up even more to avoid what he thinks is coming. So, start out with mild punishment. You can always increase the intensity if your horse is a bit numb to it, but start out with the least you can get by with and still make your point. Add your punishment in increments until you find the point where your horse understands what you want of him. You never want to start out real severe.

Check It Out

There are ways to check whether your speed control is working before your first show. Give your horse a day off. When you ride him the next day, don't go through your usual warm-up routine. Start out with a fast circle. Chase your horse around the circle at some speed. When you come across the middle and hum and he comes back to you, you know he's ready. If he can do that without any preparation, just cold out of his stall, you know your speed control is there for you when you need it.

10

LEAD CHANGES

Unlike performing high-speed circles, long sliding stops and lightning-quick turnarounds, changing leads is natural for any horse, although some are more athletic and therefore better at it than others. Watch any horse change directions at a lope in a pasture. He'll change leads every time. It's not something someone has to teach him. In riding, however, you have to create a lead-change language so your horse knows *when* you want him to change.

For some reason lead changes mystify many riders. They can't get the timing right, and they end up spurring the horse into making a change. When that happens, problems arise in a hurry. The horse gets uptight about making a lead change, bolts

Keep lead changes quiet and relaxed and your horse won't get in the bad habit of anticipating them.

TRAINER'S TIP

Simple and Flying Change

There are two types of lead changes: simple and flying. In a simple change of lead, the horse is broken down from a lope to a trot, then asked to pick up the opposite lead.

The flying lead change refers to the moment in time when horses change leads during a three-beat lope or four-beat gallop, which is in mid-stride or the suspension phase of the gait. Because all four legs are off the ground during the suspension phase, the horse appears to be "flying" through the air, hence the name.

Use your left leg to move the horse's hip to the right and open the doorway with your right leg. (In this hip control exercise, the rider exaggerates the leg cues for illustration purposes.)

through it or drags a hind lead. Neither will win any points in a reining.

In this chapter, we'll explain how to change leads, solidify them through hip-control exercises and avoid typical mistakes.

Dragging a Hind Lead

Many perfectly good reining patterns are ruined by a horse dragging or dropping a hind lead, in other words, changing in front but not behind, often called "crossfiring." It can be a real nemesis for a lot of riders. When a horse doesn't change leads behind, it costs the horse/rider duo penalties in the score.

A horse should begin a right lead by striking the ground with his left hind leg first and a left lead with his right hind leg first. (See footfall patterns for both leads in the chapter titled "Speed Control.") The following hip control exercises encourage hind-leg-first lead departures and lead changes and help prevent a horse from dropping a lead behind.

Horses that tend to change leads with their front legs first also tend to fall out of lead behind and end up crossfiring. Their shoulders dive into the lead instead of the hindquarters leading the charge. It's a very unnatural gait for the horse and difficult for the rider to sit.

Another typical time a horse falls out of lead behind is when asked to slow down from a fast circle. Many horses, especially young ones, might feel a bit unbalanced coming from a strong four-beat gallop to a slower three-beat lope. They switch the hind leg lead in an effort to steady themselves, but it backfires, and they end up moving disjointed.

Learn to avoid dragging a hind lead with the following hip control and counter-canter exercises.

Hip Control

If you can control your horse's hip, you can cause your horse to change leads. Being able to move your horse's hip to the right or left while you keep the horse's shoulders up and straight is paramount in correct lead changes.

Before you begin anything, let's review hip control, first at a standstill and then at a walk. As outlined in the chapter titled "A Solid Foundation," this should all be part of your suppling routine at the beginning of a workout anyway.

With a hand on each rein, drive your horse up into the bit, keeping the shoulders straight between the bridle reins. He should flex nicely at the poll and give you his face. The bit acts as a barrier for your horse to work behind. If he needs something more substantial, then use an arena fence as a physical block, but only until he gets the hang of it.

To move your horse's hip to the left, place your right leg behind the horse's rib cage (on his right flank) and press as you hold the reins firm. Don't use any pressure with your left leg; that doorway is open for the horse to move through. Keep pressing until the horse frees up his hindquarters (his shoulders should stay straight) and the inside hip (in this case left) moves to the left a step or two.

To move the hip to the right, place your left leg behind the horse's rib cage (or on his left flank) and press until the inside (or right) hip moves over to the right.

Practice until you can walk all around the arena or track, moving your horse's hips right and left as you walk a straight line.

Another good exercise is to hold your horse stationary with the reins to keep his front legs from moving as much as possible, and drive his hindquarters around his front end. That's a turn on the forehand — your horse moves his hind end around his front end. He isn't ready to change leads until he can do this easily in both directions.

The Counter-Canter

The single most important part of our lead-change program is teaching the horse to counter-canter, which is basically circling on the wrong lead. In other words, a horse circles to the right on a left lead and circles to the left on a right lead. (see Diagram #1.) While it sounds like an unnatural and unbalanced exercise, it's actually beneficial. As a physical exercise, the counter-canter helps to supple and strengthen your horse's body. As a mental exercise, it requires that a horse wait on you for cues. If he's not waiting, he's not obeying, and if he's not obeying, he's not reining.

The counter-canter is a natural outgrowth of hip control and probably the one best way to get a horse comfortable and relaxed about having his body parts controlled. It's the key to correct and consistent lead changes. A horse that doesn't

TRAINER'S TIP

Deadly-leaded

Horses that can change leads naturally are often referred to as "deadly-leaded" in reiner lingo. They're obviously a real plus to have in anyone's training program or in the show ring. A horse with a built-in lead-change is much easier to train for that maneuver than one on which you have to program an artificial one.

To see if a young horse, say a 2-year-old, is deadly-leaded, lope some circles and change directions from time to time. Notice whether the horse is handy enough to change leads when he changes directions.

As the horse matures and goes through more training, such as counter-cantering, he'll be able to negotiate a small circle on a wrong lead. But in the beginning you can tell if a horse is a natural lead-changer just by how he handles himself in a change of direction. Does he automatically change leads or does he remain on the same lead and lope in an awkward, stilted and uncomfortable fashion? A horse that can run, stop, turn and do all the fancy stuff but can't change leads puts you in a bad spot competitively.

DIAGRAM #1
Counter-Canter Exercise

A. Counter-canter to the left, horse is on the right lead.
B. Counter-canter to the right, horse is on the left lead.

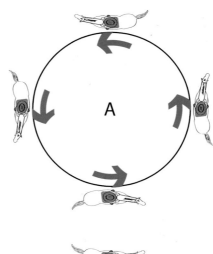

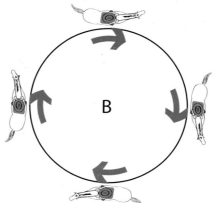

become upset with you controlling his hip movement won't get upset when you ask him to change leads either.

Your cues for the counter-canter are similar to those you used for the hip control exercise at the walk, only you're obviously at a lope.

For a counter-canter to the right, start by loping left-lead circles. Hold a rein in each hand for better control, making sure the horse keeps his shoulders up and doesn't lean into the circle. The horse's head and neck should be straight or slightly to the inside (left). As you complete the left circle, move up the center and into a right circle, but hold your horse in the same frame you had him in for the left circle. You don't want him to change leads. Keep your right leg on him to keep his hip shoved to the left. His head should still be straight or slightly tilted to the left. He's now circling right in a left lead or counter-canter.

For a counter-canter to the left, start by loping right-lead circles, keeping your horse's head straight or tilted to the right

LEAD CHANGES

To recap the footfalls of a lope: The first beat begins with the opposite hind leg striking the ground (for example, the left hind leg for a right lead). The second beat is the diagonal pair of hind and front legs (right hind leg and left front legs), and the third beat is the leading (right) front leg, followed by a moment of suspension. The lead change occurs during the moment of suspension, when the horse changes leads behind first by "switching" hips. As you view these photos, realize that each beat has different phases within the stride (from beginning to middle to end), which includes the time the feet hit the ground until they leave.

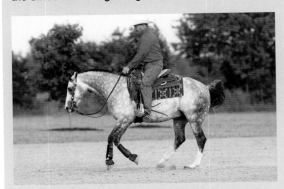

1. In the first beat of the right lead, the horse strikes off with the left hind leg. The next two feet that are about to hit the ground are the diagonal right hind and the left front.

2. In the second beat, the right hind and left front hit simultaneously. The left hind foot is at the end of its stride and the leading right foot (hence right lead) is moving forward.

3. In the third and final beat of the three-beat lope, the horse's leading right leg strikes the ground. This is the beginning phase of the third beat. The diagonal right hind and left front are at the end of their stride, and the left hind foot is lifted off the ground.

4. At the apex of the third beat, the horse bears all his weight on his leading or right leg. Note the hind legs are out behind the horse's hindquarters and that the left hind leg is leading a bit in preparation to land and begin the right lead all over again. The rider is about to cue for a change.

5. At the end of the third beat, the right or leading leg is about to be airborne and there will be a moment of suspension when the lead change occurs. Note now the right hind leg is slightly ahead of the left and about to strike next. In the previous frame his left hind leg was positioned to strike the ground first, but since the horse has been cued to change leads, he switches hips in midair (so to speak) and will come down on the opposite or right hind leg to begin the left lead.

6. The horse has successfully switched leads to the left with the right hind leg hitting the ground in the first beat. The next two legs about to strike in the second beat are the diagonal left hind and right front.

7. This is the same first beat, but near the end of that stride, where the horse propels himself forward on the right hind leg. The diagonal pair of left hind and right front legs are about to strike the ground in the second beat.

8. In the second beat of the lope, the diagonal pair (left hind and right front) are solidly bearing the horse's weight and the leading left leg extends, ready to be put down. The right hind leg is coming off the ground.

9. For the third and final beat, the left leading leg strikes the ground. The diagonal pair (right front and left hind) is about to leave the ground and the right hind leg is in the air.

10. The third beat is complete with the leading left leg lifts bearing all the horse's weight, and the other three legs are off the ground. A moment of suspension will occur when the leading left leg lifts off the ground.

DIAGRAM #2
Lead-Change Square Exercise

A. Moving in a left-hand square, depart on the right lead.

B. In the corner, make a 90-degree turn on a right-lead counter-canter.

C. Change to left lead.

D. Turn corner on left lead.

E. Change to right lead.

F. In the corner, make a 90-degree turn on a right-lead counter-canter.

G. Change to left lead.

H. Turn corner on left lead.

Change directions and perform a right-hand square with left-lead counter-canters in the designated corners (D and H).

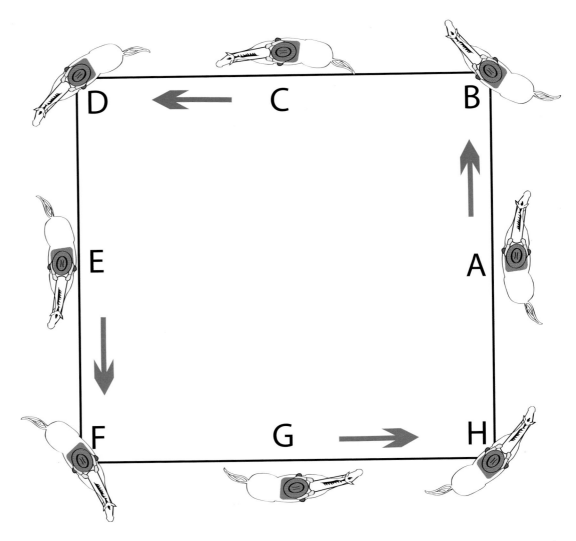

and your left leg on his left flank. Come through the middle and move into a left circle, but stay in the same right-lead frame you were in.

The first couple of times you ask for a counter-canter, your horse might change leads in the middle instead of staying in the same lead frame. Counter-cantering feels awkward to a horse, so don't punish him for it. It's no big deal if he accidentally changes without you requesting it. Ultimately, you do want him to change leads so don't get upset with him if that's what he does during the counter-canter

DIAGRAM #3
D-Shaped Circle Exercise

A. Depart on left lead on straightaway.
B. Circle to the left on left lead.
C. Cue for right lead on straightaway.
D. Circle to right on right lead.

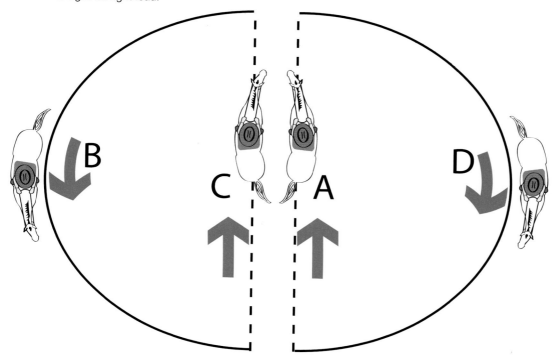

exercise. Simply go around the circle again and start over with the counter-canter.

Squares, Straight Lines and the Letter "D"

Just as having good hip control helps with performing the counter-canter, the counter-canter helps with performing correct, hind-leg-first lead changes.

To this point you've been counter-cantering in circles. Now try it in a square. The square provides you with straight lines to work along instead of circles. Changing leads on a straight-away is important for two reasons: 1) It keeps a horse's shoulders straight so the horse doesn't dive into the lead change front leg first. 2) It prevents a horse from associating a change of leads with a change of direction. This can become a bad habit, which encourages a horse to drop his shoulder to the inside.

Start by riding a square, say to the left. (See Diagram #2.) Depart into a right lead and come down the first straight line of the square in a right lead. Use your reins to make sure the horse's shoulders are up and straight. Your left leg pushes your horse's flank to the right to maintain the right lead. As you hit the corner of the square, make a somewhat sharp 90-degree turn to the left and reinforce the counter-canter by continuing to push your horse's hip to the right with your left leg.

Once you turn the corner, you're on the second straightaway of the square and set up to make a lead change to the left. Release your left leg and use your right leg to push the horse's hip to the left or inside the square. Your horse should change leads to the left.

The idea is to push, don't spur or kick your horse to change. If he doesn't change immediately, don't panic, just keep pushing and be patient. The second he does, release all leg pressure and let him lope on the left lead. Turn the corner on that lead and on the next or third straightaway, push his hip to the right again with your left leg to move into the right lead. Keep switching back and forth throughout the square. Your

1. After a lead change, in this case the horse is on the third or last beat of a right lead, ask him to slow down.

2. You break down slowly from the lope when you quit riding. Praise the horse for doing a good job.

3. The horse's reward is to relax at the walk.

horse will get pretty handy at listening to you and changing leads.

A horse has to be pretty broke in the counter-canter and in the body to be able to counter-canter the square. The turns are much sharper and your horse has to put more effort into staying in frame.

After counter-cantering and changing leads on the square, go back to circles. They should be a snap.

However, think of circles as D-shaped, not really circular. A D-shaped circle looks like a D, with one long straight line down the middle and a semi-circle connecting the ends of the straightaway. (See Diagram #3.)

Riding D-shaped circles gives you plenty of room and time to change on a straight line, just as you did in the square.

Quit Riding

A good way to keep a horse thinking "slow" during a lead change and to help prevent any charging or lead-change anticipation is to quit riding after a change. For example, lope a set of circles to the right, come down the center and change leads to the left. Lope a few more strides, then break your horse down to a trot, followed by a walk. Pet him, let him stand there and relax as a reward. This gets your horse into the mindset that lead changes are slow and unhurried, and that there's a rest period afterward. It really helps make circling maneuvers pretty to watch and also shows a horse really listening to his rider.

A lot of things happen in the center of a reining pattern, and that's where many problems crop up. Horses can get uptight about changing leads and slowing down all at the same time. Before you know it, you'll have an anxious horse and a bad habit to correct. Breaking a horse down after a change is a good insurance policy to help prevent lead-change problems in the first place.

No Spurs Allowed

Spurring your horse anywhere in the lead change is one of the worst things you can do. It's guaranteed to scare him at the very least and make him anxious or angry.

When a horse misses a lead change or drops a hind lead, take hold of him with the reins, drive him up into the bridle and keep pushing his hip over with your leg, toward the lead you want. Insist with your leg, but not your spur. You want your horse to know he messed up, and that you're going to keep pushing until he changes, but the punishment shouldn't be so severe that your horse becomes nervous. He'll quit thinking and trying after that. Hold, push and wait until he changes. When he does, release your hold and let him lope.

If he still doesn't change, break him down to a trot, push his hip over and try again.

Don't continue to gallop and let him make that mistake. Break him down and fix it. Don't get overly aggressive with him, though. Just let him know he did wrong.

If you make too big a deal out of a missed lead change and get after a horse real hard, before long he'll become upset and concerned and come through the middle running hard because he's scared of getting spurred or jerked with the reins. He'll blow right through the lead change.

Also, a horse often misses a lead because his shoulders were leaning left or right as he came down the middle or straightaway. That's why it's important to keep the horse's shoulders up and straight in any circle and during a lead change.

How Often

Work on lead changes every day and at the minimum at least two to three times a week.

Mix up your lead-change routines so your horse doesn't associate certain speeds and places in the arena where you like to change. Vary the size of circles, the straight lines and the speed at which you change. See how slow or fast your horse can go and still change. This is helpful in a show-ring situation. Whether you're loping slowly or galloping hard, you'll have the confidence in knowing your horse can perform lead changes anywhere and at any speed in the pattern.

Administer a test to your horse. Change leads through leg pressure alone; don't use both reins to steady your horse. Ride one-handed and ask for a lead change with leg pressure. If your horse responds to that degree, you're ready to show.

"Great stoppers are born to stop."

11

STOP AND BACK

Horses that are really, really good stoppers are that way from Day One. Physically and mentally, they were born to stop. It's easy for them. Modern reining horse breeding programs excel at producing competitive reiners. A horse that's bred to do the job makes training much more simple and enjoyable for both you and the horse.

On a great stopping horse, it seems that when you pick up the reins your hand is connected to the horse's hocks and the horse stops. The stop is almost automatic on the good ones. All you have to do is stay out of the horse's way and let him do it. Not all horses are that talented, however, and no matter what, you still have to teach them *when* to stop.

In this chapter, we'll talk about how to achieve the attack-the-ground kind of stop that scores points in a reining, as well as the correct back-up.

Stopping Style

Stopping style is a big consideration in selecting a reining horse. The way a horse stops naturally is what you've got to work with. You can improve on it somewhat, but many times what you see is what you get. You can ruin one by trying to change what comes naturally.

Besides being unique to each horse, stopping style is a big factor in how a horse is judged. A horse that holds his head high in a stop usually skates on the slide plates, thus staying on top of the dirt, much the way reining horses did it in the past. This type of stop doesn't earn as many points as those performed by today's top horses. A great stopper literally attacks the ground. He lowers his neck and brings up his back as his hind legs fold underneath him. They hold the ground while his front legs pedal for more ground. He still slides a long way, like the skater, but it's deep, as if the horse were plowing a furrow in the arena dirt. This is the kind winning today.

It's worth noting that a horse's hindquarter conformation often dictates how he stops. A horse with strong hindquarters and straight hind legs generally stops deep and straight. One whose hind legs toe out might stop with one or both hind feet out to the side. A horse with weak hindquarters and/or toe-in hind legs might stop very narrow and almost hit his front feet with his hind feet.

However, some horses with poor hindquarter conformation, such as being post-legged (no angulation between the hock and cannon bone), can be awesome stoppers and still stay sound. That goes back

Good reining horses learn to love putting on the brakes.

TRAINER'S TIP

Boot Up

When you practice stopping, it's very important to put protective leg gear on your horse, both skid boots and bell boots. When he gets deep in the ground, your horse might burn his hind fetlocks or accidentally step on his shoe and rip off part of his hoof or bruise or cut the bulbs of his heels. Either way, it could be a long time before his legs are in good enough shape to go again. Even if he's not visibly hurt, he could be so sore that he quits stopping for you.

Bell boots help protect the horse's front heels from being clipped during hard, sliding stops.

to the horse's heart and desire that we talked about at the beginning of this book. If a horse wants to stop, he'll do it no matter what.

Brake Controls

Before we get into the mechanics of stopping, let's review the basic brake controls mentioned in the chapter titled "A Solid Foundation." We teach our horses to stop using three cues — two physical and one verbal. The physical cues include rein pressure (pulling back on the reins) and lack of leg pressure (releasing all leg pressure and pushing feet forward in the stirrups). The traditional verbal cue is simply "whoa."

It's a good idea to use all three, especially in the beginning stages of your stopping program. You can refine the maneuver by just using one cue at a time. You'll find your horse responding to any of the cues individually. That comes in handy in show situations. For example, if you're in a noisy arena and lucky enough to have the audience cheering for you, your horse might not hear you say "whoa" but he'll feel rein pressure or your feet moving forward in your stirrups. It's nice to have that kind of insurance.

The verbal cue "whoa" is universal in the world of horses. It's traditionally used to ask a horse to stop what he's doing and don't move. And that's the effect we want here. To cement it in your horse's mind, use the two physical cues below in conjunction with the word "whoa." When your horse comes to a stop, back him a step or two. Allow the horse to settle and relax as his reward. It won't be long before your horse hunts the word "whoa," and you won't even need the physical cues.

There's no better feeling than walking to the center of the pen to begin your run in a horse show, saying "whoa" and having your horse stop and take a step back and relax. You know your horse is on your team that day because he's already come back to you. He's thinking about you.

With the rein pressure cue, take the slack out of the reins with a soft, steady motion and keep your hands as low as possible, no higher than the saddle horn. You can even put your rein hand down on the horse's mane. When your horse begins to stop, release all pressure. Give him back the slack immediately. You do this enough times and your horse will start committing his hind legs to the ground in a stop the second he feels you pick up the slack. You won't need to get to the bit; your horse will already be stopped. It'll appear as if you shoved the reins to your horse — something you see top reiners do in a show. They look as if they're throwing the reins to the horse as he stops, not pulling back on him. The timing is quick, but it's the timing that gives the horse the instantaneous reward for stopping.

Snatching or jerking the reins to make your horse stop causes head-position problems, so keep the reins soft and low. A martingale can be helpful if your horse wants to carry his head a bit high. The martingale gives you some leverage and puts the horse in the correct frame for stopping.

If your horse raises his head after a stop, keep ahold of him with the reins and flutter your legs along his sides until he drops his head. You want him to learn to stop with his head down, not up in the air. When his head comes down, his back comes up and he's better able to get his hind feet underneath himself. When his head goes up, his back hollows, making it very hard to use his hind legs effectively in a stop.

The second physical cue is to release any leg pressure you might have had on your horse as he's running down to the stop and shove your feet forward in the stirrups. In effect, you quit riding and are asking your horse to quit as well. In the first part of this cue you obviously aren't asking him to move fast anymore, and the second part is a signal to slow down and stop.

When you shove your feet forward, you'll find yourself naturally sitting back a bit farther, which all works well in a hard stop. You don't ever want to be leaning forward when your horse comes to a stop. It'll throw you out of the saddle and off balance. Not a pretty sight to the judge. Therefore, in a stop, the correct position for your seat is back, a little behind the horse's motion. Also, having your feet forward helps you brace for the big stops.

As far as the sequence of cues goes, "whoa" comes first, followed by picking up your rein hand and pushing out your feet. The later two happen simultaneously. It's important to give the cues in this order because the word "whoa" is the catalyst for the stop. Think of stopping as you would a car with brake fluid. If you're running down to a stop and you've already picked up the reins, it's as if you're running down with your hand on the brake when you say "whoa." Chances are your horse isn't going to feel much when you say "whoa" to him. You have only so much brake fluid.

Fencing

Fencing is a technique that introduces horses to the act of stopping. Reiners use a fence or a gate as a barricade beyond which the horse can't go. It provides three benefits: 1) The horse learns to stop without having to be pulled on. 2) It encourages the horse to use his hind legs in a sliding motion, and 3) it tackles "scotching" problems. (A horse is said to "scotch" when he sets up and tries to stop before you ask him.)

Fencing any horse, but especially a young one, should be done slowly and in a relaxed manner. Simply lope quietly up to the fence and let it stop your horse. Don't gallop fast,

In an attack-the-ground type of stop, the horse plows deep furrows with his hind legs as his front legs pedal for more ground.

at this point, and don't go back and forth a dozen times asking for a hard stop. That's for horses much farther along in their training. You might finish your training session with a fencing stop. Lope up to the arena fence and ask your horse to stop. If he puts on the brakes, get off and call it a day.

In teaching your horse to fence, hold a rein in each hand to help keep your horse straight. He might try to fishtail around, but his body needs to be straight to stop correctly.

About 10 feet from the fence, say "whoa" and allow the fence to stop the horse. Just stand there and let it sink into your horse that when he stops, he gets to relax.

At the fence, make a turn or two or walk a small circle before you head back the other

To stop using all three brake controls, say "whoa," lean back, shove your feet forward in the stirrups and use rein pressure.

In this three-quarter front view, it's obvious how much the rider's leg pressure in the stirrups buffers the shock of the deep stop. Also, notice how far the horse's hind legs are underneath the horse's body. A horse almost "breaks in two" to accomplish this kind of stop.

A martingale is useful for head positioning in the early phases of a stopping program.

direction. Try to keep things quiet and prevent your horse from anticipating what happens next.

During the rundown between the fences, it's important to keep your horse straight. If he veers off course, bring him back, softly, not abruptly, just put him back in place on the straight line you intended. This is all in preparation for the eventual rundown to a hard, sliding stop, where you want your horse to stay between the reins and stop straight. This is where he learns to stay straight.

Good fencing sets the stage for good stops. Later on, when you add speed, it's not confusing for your horse. He knows how to run up to the fence; and he knows that once he gets there, if he stays straight, he'll get to rest for a second.

The All-Important Rundown

A good stop almost always comes after a good rundown. The rundown builds momentum, and it's the momentum that carries the horse through to a spectacular stop. Without momentum, horses run through a stop or just dribble down to a point-subtracting halt.

To gain momentum, think of shifting gears on a car. For a smooth ride, you'd go from first, to second, third and finally fourth. You wouldn't skip the second gear and shift into fourth. The same with a horse. Ask him to increase his speed incrementally, so that he doesn't miss a gear. Only that way can he build momentum to a stop. Don't hold your horse to a slow lope, then ask him to blast from first to fourth. His stop will be out of control and probably ratty-looking, if he stops at all.

Should your horse, on his own, blast from a lower gear to a higher one during the rundown, pull him into the ground. Don't necessarily punish him, but stop him in his tracks. Start over again and pull him back down if he remains chargey. You want the gears the horse goes through in his speed build-up to be sequential — not first, second, fourth, but first, second, third, then fourth.

A horse with a gear-skipping problem might possibly need a lot of work. Just pulling him into the ground one time isn't enough for a particularly hard-charging horse. You might have to wear out a pair of sliders getting the problem fixed. But don't let a chargey finish to the stop, or you will have taught him to do just that. Instead, take hold of the reins, stop his forward momentum and ride him in a tight circle. Keep cir-

TRAINER'S TIP

Scotching

You'll find that after you show your horse a half dozen or more times, he knows when the stops happen. He might start anticipating them and "scotch" or stop before you ask him.

At home in practice or, better yet, at a schooling show, the second you feel him scotch on you, kick him through the stop and all the way to the fence. Let the fence stop him. That teaches him to wait on your signal to stop. You might blow the schooling class, but that's what they're for. You might even have to sacrifice a class at a weekend show to resolve the problem in your horse's mind; but you have no choice, you have to fix it.

cling until the horse comes back to you and resumes the speed you want. Or you can stop him, spin him 180 degrees and lope back the opposite direction.

If your horse makes a mistake on the rundown, let him. You can't fix a problem until one is presented to you. Only by making mistakes and you showing the way will a horse learn his job. For example, if he leans to the right or left, steer him back on track, then leave him alone. Don't make a big deal out of it, but let him know he did wrong and put him back where you want him.

If he continues leaning, stop him and correct him by spinning him 360 degrees, then continue on in the same direction. By making that type of correction then, you make an impression and won't have to keep doing it all day long. If he leans to the left, spin him to the right and vice versa. Always take him in the direction opposite of the way he wants to go.

Horses have preferred leads and stop better on one than the other. Practice both leads equally on your rundowns. On a left-lead rundown, keep your right leg on your horse to make sure the right hip is up under him and vice versa for a right-lead rundown.

The Stop

Remember that fencing is a tool many reiners use to accustom their horses to stopping, but don't use it as a crutch. At some point, your horse needs to know how to stop without one, on your command anywhere and any time.

With that in mind, after a few good fencing stops, ask for a stop in the middle of the pen. Use both your verbal "whoa" and the rein and leg cues. When your horse stops, back a few steps and let him rest. Build from there. Stop in

RUNDOWN, STOP AND BACK

1. *The rider builds momentum in the rundown.*

2. *The horse's body is straight throughout the rundown.*

3. *The rider sits back and asks the horse to stop.*

4. *The horse responds by gathering himself and committing his hind legs to the ground, in this case the right hind first.*

5. *Both hind legs are now committed to the ground, but the horse still pedals in front.*

6. *The horse's hind legs dig farther underneath as the horse's front end keeps up the pedaling motion.*

various places in your arena or on your track. Mix it up to keep your horse listening to you.

In the beginning, your horse was probably a tad frightened when his hind legs slipped out from underneath him in a stop. Slide plates have that effect. But by now, it's become a game for your horse and most learn to enjoy putting on the brakes. As your horse gains confidence in locking up his hind end and sliding along the ground, he'll go farther

7. At the beginning of the slide, you can start to see the back of the saddle and saddle pad lift as the horse's hindquarters come into full lockdown.

8. The horse keeps sliding...

9. and sliding...

10. and finally comes to a complete stop. Notice how far under himself the horse is by the big gap between the saddle, pad and horse's back.

11. The horse has stood up and is taking a few steps backward. Note the diagonal right front and left rear legs are working in unison in a correct two-beat back-up.

and put more effort into it, and start pedaling with his front legs. When he does, reward him. Pet him and let him rest, but not very long. If a horse associates stopping with getting to rest, he might start charging to his stops in anticipation of the long rest. Sometimes you create your own problems when all you're trying to do is reward your horse. What you've taught the horse, in effect, is that the faster he gets from Point A to Point B to stop, the longer he gets to rest. So, reward him, yes, but not for an extended period of time.

One thing you can do after a good stop is to simply walk your horse in a small circle. He can get his air and relax, but he doesn't think he's through for the day. You're resting him, but not really resting him. You can do things such as making sure he's soft in the face by asking him to give to rein pressure — just a little reminder. Your horse will realize he's still in his work clothes and his attitude will stay good and focused.

On the other hand, if your horse takes repeated encouragement from you just to make it through a rundown, maybe you should reward him by giving him a long rest.

For a horse that won't keep his hocks in the ground during a stop, lift the reins high after he stops. This lifts the horse's head, neck and shoulders and consequently his front end. When the front end comes up, the hind end goes down. Start again and ask for another stop.

Fencing is a handy tool in any stopping program.

Some extremely lazy horses need different motivation than those with a lot of get-up-and-go.

Troubleshooting the Stop

As with any maneuver, problems will arise during the training process. In stopping, the two most common errors are running through a stop and coming out of one. The corrections for both problems are similar. They're based on reminding the horse that he must give to the bit.

For a horse that runs through a stop, take both reins and pull him into the ground. Don't let him continue to take the bit and run. Once he's stopped, back him a few steps and lift his shoulders with the reins at the same time. He should give in the poll. You are correcting him at the same time you're asking him to give to the bit.

In the second stopping error, the horse doesn't use his hocks to stay in the ground and ends up hopping or coming out of his stops. Lope him and ask for a stop with your reins the way you normally would — low and a pull backward. After he stops, raise your reins high, toward his ears, and ask him to back. This lifts the horse's head, which in turn lifts the horse's front end and consequently his hind end is down.

In either scenario, it's not a snatch or jerk on the reins, which would scare your horse and make him apprehensive about stopping in the future. After repeated jerks for missed stops, your horse will begin to associate the word "whoa" with painful jerking and he'll raise his head in anticipation. Then you'll have a head-position problem. The pull is more of a lift of the reins. As the horse steps backward, you sort of "zip up" the front end. His head, neck, shoulders and front legs literally elevate and his hindquarters drop. You'll find your horse with his hocks deep in the ground and he'll get lighter and lighter in your hands. Lope off again and ask for another stop. See if the lifting fix cures the problem. Keep at it until the horse stays light on his front end and holds the ground in a stop.

Back-up

Every NRHA pattern calls for a stop followed by a back-up. Not all stops require a back-up, but every back-up is preceded by a stop. There are good reasons to teach a horse to take a few steps backward after a stop. For one thing, backing helps keep the hindquarters underneath the horse's body, thus making stops easier to perform and therefore prettier to the judge. As the horse comes to a stop, he thinks "back" and his hind legs move under his body. Having his hindquarters somewhat lower than his forequarters puts him in a good framework to stop, so the two work hand-in-hand, so to speak. Also, the stop and back-up become one smooth, seamless motion — another point-attracting maneuver.

Taking a few steps backward after a practice stop is one thing, but you'll need to ask your horse to do a lot more in a pattern. In a show situation, you might have to back the length of half an arena (or at least 10 feet as the patterns require)! That means your horse will have to move backward as easily and willingly as he goes forward. That requires a little practice.

Backing is one of the basics we touched on in "A Solid Foundation." To review, after a stop, when your horse's hindquarters are still

Stop a horse that leans on the reins by turning or spinning him 360 degrees and starting over. Don't let a chargey or crooked horse continue to run down to a stop.

Ask your horse for a "show stop" only once or twice a week. You don't want to run out of brake fluid by overstopping a good thing.

in a crouching position, maintain a steady pull on the reins. That prevents your horse from coming out of the stop and going forward. He'll search for a way to get some relief from the rein pressure. When he eventually takes a step backward, release your reins and let him stand. That's his reward.

In the beginning, accept a step or two, but keep working on this procedure day after day, asking for more steps incrementally, and your two steps will turn into 20. Realize that it might take two months for that, but that's okay.

Straightness is the Key

The trick in backing is to keep your horse straight. Straightness or crookedness in your horse's body becomes readily apparent when he backs. A body that's straight through the head, neck, shoulders, back and hindquarters backs in a straight line. If any body part is stuck out or leans, the horse backs crookedly.

Think of the horse's body as a swivel. Whatever the front end does, the hind end does in the opposite direction. For example, if the horse leans with his right shoulder, his hindquarters swing left and he'll back toward the left. But if his left shoulder leans, he'll back toward the right.

To look at it and say it another way, a horse backs in the direction his hip leans. If his hip leans to the right, he'll back to the right and vice-versa.

To keep your horse straight, maintain steady pressure on your reins, but use your leg on the side the horse is backing crookedly. When he backs left, use your left leg behind the cinch to move the horse back to the right or center. If his hindquarters move to the right, use your right leg behind the cinch until he moves back to the center.

Done correctly, there's a cadence in backing. The horse's legs move in a two-beat synchronization, much like a trot backward. The right front leg moves in unison with the left hind and the left fore with the right hind. Any other version of leg movement means the horse isn't moving correctly. He's a bit sticky and possibly leaning one direction or the other.

Add Speed Slowly

Speed in the back-up comes like it does with every other maneuver — over time. Don't ask for speed until your horse is moving

correctly backward for at least a dozen steps. Once he's got the footwork down, then use a verbal cue, such a clucking sound or whatever you use to ask for speed.

Don't ask for a fast back-up every day. Backing up isn't a natural movement for a horse. A horse would rarely, if ever, back up in pasture or out in the wild. Your horse might resent it if you keep pushing him to do it. It's something you can work on a couple of times a week. Do get a few back-up steps after a stop, as you would during a normal stopping practice, but don't ask for a speedy back-up on a daily basis.

The Show Stop

Along the same lines, you might work on your horse's stop anywhere from a dozen to two dozen times in a typical training session, but don't require a maxed-out effort on each stop. Just look for correctness in your horse's head, shoulders, hocks, etc. You want your horse to run and stop straight, and you can check a lot of that out at a slow lope rather than an all-out gallop.

Once you're satisfied that all stopping systems are go, ask for a "show stop," one in which your horse has to put in a real effort, the kind you want in a show situation. However, perform this kind of stop only once or twice a week. You don't want to burn your horse out, but at the same time you need to know what he's got. On a young horse, say a 3-year-old, you could back off for a couple of weeks if he's stopping hard correctly and consistently. Closer to futurity time, step up the program a bit to keep him sharp on his stops. The rest of the time work to maintain correct form in the stop as well as the back-up.

"The horse literally rolls back over his hocks."

12

ROLLBACK

As a maneuver, the rollback is aptly named. It's a 180-degree turn on the haunches in which a horse literally rolls back over his hocks and goes the opposite direction. Like the back-up, the rollback in a reining pattern always occurs after a stop. The change of direction sets the horse up for his rundown to another stop.

Walk Before You Run

While the snappy, crowd-pleasing, point-getting rollbacks you see at a horse show take place after sliding stops, don't start there to teach the rollback to your horse. Instead, work on the maneuver from a walk because it's easier for your horse to understand the concept at a slower speed.

During basic training, you introduced your horse to rolling back over his hocks alongside a fence (see "A Solid

After a stop, the rollback sets up the horse for the next rundown to another stop.

117

1. *In the early phases of teaching the rollback, stop and take a few steps backward. Then turn the horse's head in the direction of the rollback.*

2. *The inside front leg is the first to move, followed by the outside front.*

Foundation"). There you walked or trotted him in small circles and turned him into the fence. The limited space available for the turn encouraged the horse to collect himself over his hocks and spin back on his tracks, thus performing the elements of a rollback.

In the round pen, you used forward motion to accomplish that basic rollback and you will again when you work on the maneuver in your arena or on your slide track. It'll seem contradictory, though, because this time you'll actually teach the rollback from a back-up. However, it's the forward motion out of the back-up that propels you out of the turn.

Back Up to Rollback

Just as backing after a stop helps position your horse's hind legs for the stop (as explained in the previous chapter), backing also helps position your horse for a rollback. With his hocks in motion backing up, the horse places his hind legs where they need to be for this maneuver — under his body. Here's the sequence.

Walk your horse forward and stop him. Using both reins, ask him for a few steps back. Tip your horse's nose in the direction you want to roll back, support the turn with the outside or neck rein across the horse's neck, and use leg pressure to move his body

in that direction. Cluck or use a verbal cue to ask for forward motion and drive the horse out of the rollback. The result should be a turn over the haunches or rollback.

For example, to roll back to the left, come to a stop, back a few steps, pick up your left rein to tip the horse's nose to the left, use your right rein across the horse's neck and apply right leg pressure on the horse's rib-cage. Smooch or cluck for forward motion. The horse should roll back over his hocks and make the turn.

To roll back to the right, back up, then tip your horse's nose to the right with your right rein, place your left rein across his neck and use left-leg pressure on his rib cage to encourage him to move right. Cluck or smooch.

The horse's body alignment should be straight during the rollback, with just his nose tipped toward the inside. If your horse over-bends into the rollback, with his body more in a C-shape, his inside shoulder won't be in position to allow his inside front leg to lead into the rollback (see below).

Correct Footwork

In the beginning stages of teaching this maneuver, make sure your horse's footwork is correct. The inside front leg should be the first to move in the direction of the rollback. It

3. *The horse rolls over his hocks as he completes the rollback.*

rollback after every stop. While you want him light you don't want him doing anything on his own, so from time to time, just stop and stand still. Let him relax and don't roll back.

When your horse can stop, back up freely and roll back consistently after you lay your outside leg on him, he's ready to step up to trying it at a lope and then at the gallop.

Rolling back out of a sliding stop is the ultimate goal but realize that it adds a degree of difficulty because now speed is a factor. The horse's adrenaline increases the faster he runs. That's why it's so important to have the footwork down at slower speeds.

Correct Lead

Your horse should lope, not burst, out of the rollback. Bursting out of the rollback can cause you to get on the wrong lead or over-spin the rollback and be off pattern.

If you've followed the hand and leg cues correctly, your horse should come out of the rollback on the correct lead going into the next stop. This is important in a reining pattern, which requires you to be on the correct lead at the top of the rundown to a stop. You won't incur any penalties if you come out of the rollback on a wrong lead, but if you don't change it before the top of the rundown, you will. It's always better and presents a prettier picture to the judge to come out of the rollback on the correct lead.

Timing is Everything

One of the most important things in a rollback is the timing of when to ask for it. After a horse stops, especially after a big sliding stop, his hind legs are deep underneath him, sometimes so far they're almost under his shoulders. With his hindquarters so low to the ground, he's definitely out of position to roll back at that moment. It takes the horse a second or two to straighten his hocks enough so he can perform the maneuver. Otherwise, he might make a U-turn instead of a snappy rollback. He doesn't need to stand totally square on his hind legs; he'll still be in somewhat of a crouching position. But he must be able to stand up enough to have the strength and power to drive himself out of the turn, so wait to ask him to roll back until after you feel he's righted himself.

Fix Those Leaks

Horses leak out (stop short of the full 180-degree rollback) because they lack forward

reaches to the inside, while the outside front leg steps across. The outside hind leg moves around the relatively stationary inside hind leg. This step-across motion is a forerunner to the turnaround, addressed in the next chapter.

The horse's front feet should be on the ground, stepping across one another, not hopping around the hind feet. Hopping is often caused by the rider jerking the reins and using spurs too abruptly in cuing the horse. That scares the horse, who, in turn, hops around in anticipation of the jerk or spur. Instead, he should sweep low across the ground with his front feet. You'll get this by keeping your cues quiet. The more the horse keeps his legs on the ground, the quicker he is and the prettier the rollback will be.

Once the horse is comfortable with the maneuver at a walk, go to the trot. Trot the horse straight forward, ask him to stop, back up and roll back in the opposite direction. However, try not to trot the horse out of the rollback. He should either walk out quietly or move up into the lope.

Practice the rollback at the slower speeds going in both directions. As an exercise, walk all over your arena asking your horse to roll back every 10 to 20 feet. He'll become very light in your hands and start anticipating the

ROLLBACK

1. The horse lopes along the fence in a right lead.

2. The rider asks for a stop.

3. The horse's hind legs move deep underneath his body...

4. ...and deeper still.

5. The rider waits for the horse to stand back up before he asks the horse to roll back to the left. Note the left inside front leg is about to be picked up.

6. The horse begins the rollback with his inside front (or left) leg.

motion. Their energy just dies out and they often make U-turns instead of rollbacks.

When that happens, pull the horse through the rest of the turn with your reins and boot him up into a lope. Make him jet out of there

and not be lazy about it. You're training the horse to think that he must always go all the way through the turn, not just partway.

Another technique is to complete a circle or 360-degrees, not simply the 180 degrees

7. *The outside front (or right) leg is about to move next.*

8. *The outside front leg prepares to cross over the inside front.*

9. *The outside (or right) hind leg is about to pick up.*

10. *The horse bears most of his weight on the inside (or left) hind leg as he reaches out with his left front leg.*

11. *The horse's left front leg accepts more of his weight in the left rollback.*

12. *The horse pushes off on his right hind leg as he begins the left lead in this left rollback sequence.*

required in the maneuver. There are two good reasons for this. One is that while he's spinning, the horse is keeping his legs on the ground, which is all part of proper step-across footwork in a rollback. Second, in a show situation, you'll lose about 20 to 30 percent of your efficiency (the rollback movement) due to typical show pressures, jitters, rider error, etc. So, if during practice you don't complete the 360 degrees, you might find your horse

After a stop, allow the horse to regain his footing behind so he can power out of the rollback.

not completing the full 180 degrees during a reining pattern. He'll come up short and you'll lose points.

To vary the exercise, spin 360 degrees, then another 180 degrees and face the opposite direction, which is the correct direction for a 180-degree rollback. In other words, you spin 1 ½ times around. Because you've kept your horse guessing, he won't anticipate stopping too early and jumping out of the rollback. He'll wait until you drive him out of there.

When you do want a 180-degree rollback, shut the horse down by putting your rein hand down toward his mane. Lowering the rein hand is a standard cue to slow down, and the horse stops his motion when he feels it.

Lean No More

Correctly executed, a rollback is a turn toward the wall, fence or rail, depending on where you perform your pattern. After a while, your horse can get very wise to that scenario and try to outthink you. He'll start getting in a hurry and lean toward the wall. When a horse leans on the rundown to a stop you're just about guaranteed a crooked stop, so it's something you want to nip in the bud right away.

You can help circumvent that by mixing up the direction you turn. From time to time, turn him to the inside. Keep him waiting on you and guessing what you'll ask for. This also helps keep your horse quiet so he doesn't charge out of his rollbacks. He'll remain attentive to you.

After a good stop and rollback, break your horse down to a trot and then stop a few strides out. Let him relax and catch his breath. That's the best reward you can give your horse for a job well done.

"It's one of the reining horse's signature maneuvers."

13

TURNAROUND

A turnaround (or spin) is a complete 360-degree turn on the haunches, in which the horse plants an inside hind foot and his other three feet revolve around it. It's a spectacular maneuver, one of the reining horse's signature movements like the sliding stop — performed fast and smooth. The faster and smoother the turnaround, the better it is and the more points it earns.

All reining patterns call for a set of turnarounds in each direction and they are judged separately. You can plus (score points) a set of right spins but minus the left ones if your horse jumps out of them or over- or under-spins.

Horses seem to favor one direction, much like they do one lead over another, so you might have to work on one side more than the other. However, your goal is to have mirror-image turnarounds.

The incredible athleticism of the reining horse is evident in a dynamic turnaround.

125

Like the rollback, turnarounds are achieved through forward motion and proper footwork. In this chapter, we discuss the footwork pattern, offer handy exercises for speed and accuracy and explain how to troubleshoot some common problems.

Footwork First

As stated above, in a turnaround, the horse pivots off an inside hind foot. It's okay if the hind foot moves a little, but it shouldn't jump around much as the horse travels. You can prevent that by first teaching your horse

Walk your horse in a small circle with a rein in each hand. Lay the outside rein against his neck and tip his nose to the inside with your inside rein.

The inside front leg moves first so the…

the outside front leg can cross over.

proper footwork, which is a step-over or cross-over motion.

Like other maneuvers, approach your turn-around training program slowly. Walking and then trotting in small circles is the best way to help your horse get his footwork down. While those two gaits are slow, they still provide the forward momentum you need for the lateral sweeping motion of a turnaround.

The cues are similar to those you used in teaching the rollback. In fact, one of the rollback exercises (see the chapter titled "Rollback") had you turning 360 degrees in an effort to sharpen the horse's footwork as well as teach the horse to finish the rollback turn and not come up short. The basic elements of the turnaround shouldn't be foreign to your horse at this stage of the game. You're simply building on steps you've already completed in his training program.

With a hand on each rein, walk the horse in a small circle. Lay the outside rein (indirect or neck-rein) against your horse's neck and pick up the inside (direct) rein to tip the horse's nose or chin to the inside. That also moves the inside front leg out of the way, so the outside front leg can cross over. The correct footfall pattern is to have the outside leg move across, not behind, the inside leg. A horse loses forward motion (and therefore speed) when he crosses under, not over, his

inside leg. If that happens, move your horse out of the turnaround and start again. Don't let him cultivate that bad habit.

Take your inside leg off the horse's inside rib cage to open the door and put your outside leg on the horse's outside rib cage to push the horse's body over. As with

A view of the crossover from behind.

Getting the footwork right is crucial in a turnaround, otherwise speed and smoothness suffer.

all maneuvers you've done, the outside leg encourages the horse to move away from pressure. When he takes one crossover step (the outside leg crosses over the inside leg), release everything and let him walk out of it. That's his reward.

After a few days of getting one crossover step, go for two, then three and up, but do so slowly and incrementally, so your horse never gets stressed by the maneuver. Forget about speed at this point. Just go for slow and correct crossover steps.

In the beginning, it helps if you hold your inside rein a bit higher than your outside rein so you can pick up the inside shoulder and direct it.

Walk all over your track or arena crossing over one or two steps and then walking out, crossing over and then walking out to solidify the footwork for your horse. When

A horse really reaches with his front legs in a turnaround.

The horse pivots around his inside hind leg.

he's comfortable with the maneuver and consistent in his responses, move up into a trot. The trot is a good gait to train from because the short two-stride steps have a lot of rhythm and cadence to them, which helps in the step-across motion of a turnaround.

Here are the mechanics of a left and then right turnaround at the trot.

For a left turnaround, jog or trot slowly in a small left circle. Pick up your reins in two hands to steer the horse. Lay the outside (right) or neck-rein against the horse's neck and pull the inside or left (direct) rein to the left. The sequence is outside rein, inside rein. Open up your left leg and apply pressure on the horse's rib cage with your right leg.

Your horse should turn tightly to the left in the beginnings of a left turnaround. Make one complete revolution, then trot out in a small, left circle again.

For a right turnaround, trot a small right circle. Lay your outside (left) or neck-rein against the horse's neck and pick up the inside right rein to turn right. Remove any inside or right leg pressure and place your left or outside leg on the horse's left rib cage. Have him turn 360 degrees to the right and then trot out in another right circle.

Repeat in both directions all over your arena. Do this until your horse reacts to your neck-rein immediately and turns the second you pick up the neck-rein to lay it against his neck.

Neck-rein Response

Notice that through repetition, your horse learns to respond to the neck-rein first. You can eventually drop the inside rein when you go to riding one-handed, which is the ultimate objective.

One important note: Don't lay your indirect neck-rein across the horse's neck; lay it against the horse's neck. They are two different things. When you lay it across the neck, you literally cross the midline of the horse's neck with your hand and this puts the horse's head and neck out of position. His head tilts toward the outside, which is the opposite of what you want. Laying the rein against the neck is like creating a wall or barrier. The horse's head remains straight and he moves away from the rein pressure.

Mix up things a bit to help sharpen your horse's responses to the neck-rein and the turnaround. One good exercise is to reverse the rein pressure in the small circle. For example, in a left circle, pick up the reins but instead of continuing the turn to the left, turn your horse to the right by laying the new outside rein (left rein) on his neck and pulling on the new inside or right rein. Your horse will roll over his hocks and go into a right turnaround. Then trot out to the right.

Some horses get a "rubber neck" during turnaround training sessions. A horse might give his head all the way, but his feet still go straight and he doesn't turn. To correct that, take the inside or direct rein and pull the horse's head back tightly toward your knee. Use outside leg pressure to reinforce your cue if necessary. That forces the horse's inside front leg to step back, and, when it does, the rest of his body will follow. When he takes that step back, turn loose your rein pressure.

Go Slow to Go Fast

In the early stages, ask for just one complete revolution in a turnaround, then trot out as quietly as you trotted into the circle. As your horse becomes more confident and relaxed in this maneuver, continue asking him to turn two or three times, then trot out

Lay the neck-rein against the horse's neck, not across it.

The horse's neck should remain relatively straight during the turnaround, but you should be able to see the corner of his eye. His inside ear might dip toward the inside of the turn.

of it. Don't demand a half dozen or more tight turns in the beginning. You'll only scare your horse. When your horse is in the proper turnaround frame, you'll see his inside eye and jaw. His inside ear will drop some as he gives on the side he's turning on.

Don't worry about where your horse's hind feet are at this time and don't worry about speed. Both will come as your horse gets his front footwork down, which he'll do with the above exercises. They teach him where to put his feet in a steady rhythm and cadence. Until that's automatic, don't bother with speed.

Multiple Revolutions

By the time you start asking for multiple revolutions in your turnaround, your horse has trotted in and out of them for quite some time, so he's prepared to step up a bit. (On a 2-year-old, that could be at least a year to a year and a half.)

To this point, you've used walking and trotting as your forward momentum into the turnaround, but now you'll need to advance your horse to perform the maneuver from a standstill. He should understand the cues you've given him and make the transition nicely.

Hold the reins in both hands on either side of the saddle horn about 2 inches above the horse's neck, just like you did at a walk and trot. The cues are the same.

To turn to the left, lay your right rein against the horse's neck. Your horse should make some effort to move away from the rein and turn to the left. If he doesn't, "bite" (tug) on the left rein slightly, not hard, just enough to say "Come on." As soon as he moves to the left, release your rein pressure.

You want the horse to continue turning to the left. It doesn't have to be fast, just a slow, quiet turn to the left, with his left hind leg planted. You shouldn't have to apply pressure with your reins or legs. Just let the horse turn of his own accord, until you tell him to stop.

If the horse comes out of the turn or stops on his own, "bite" him again with the reins and maybe even bump his rib cage with your outside leg. If you still don't get the required reaction, press your spur into your horse until you get a reaction. Then, return him to the same position and start again. Punish him every time he quits the turnaround. He'll learn that the best place to be is in the turnaround until you take him out of it.

To turn to the right, reverse the procedure.

Practice this exercise around 10 times per session until your horse is solid in it. All you want to have to do is use outside rein pressure and have your horse keep turning until you say "whoa."

Speed comes as your horse becomes more confident in his footwork.

Add Speed

To speed up the turnaround, cluck or kiss to your horse, whatever cue you use for speed, and ask for a higher gear than the slow turn you've been getting. If that doesn't work, slap the horse's outside shoulder with your reins to encourage him to hustle.

With speed, things can start to fall apart. The horse might lose form or jump out of the turn; this time you've got to be more serious in making your point. Take a firm rein hold, trot the horse in a tight circle while bumping him off the bridle several times until you feel him soften. But don't punish your horse in the spin; take him out it to correct him. You don't want him to associate the act of spinning with punishment. You want him to hunt the spin spot and stay there.

Once you've corrected the horse, allow him to stand still and soak in the situation, or ponder the point. Then start again and ask for speed.

The Shut-off

Turnarounds must be precise in a reining pattern. Depending on the pattern, there are usually four or four and a quarter turns in each direction. You'll lose points for over- or under-spinning, so the shut-off for the turnaround becomes very important.

As in the stop, the magic word here is "whoa." It should mean only one thing to

After a good effort, let your horse stand, relax and catch his breath.

the horse — cease all motion, stop whatever you're doing.

When you utter the sacred word, also lower your rein hand toward or on the mane. That's also a signal to stop. Leaving your rein hand up could cause some confusion to the horse, who might go the other way or back up. So lower your rein hand when you say whoa. After the shut-off, let the horse relax for a few minutes and get his air.

There will be times when your horse feels something and thinks it's a cue to

To shut off the turnaround, say "whoa" and lower your rein hand to the horse's neck.

stop. Maybe you've shifted in the saddle or fixed your reins. He might become confused and think you've asked for a stop. Punish him for this. Bite with the reins or use your spurs. He shouldn't ever stop until you give him the command.

For a horse who doesn't listen to the magic word and shut down the turnaround, let him make the mistake, but immediately punish him by pulling him the other direction and getting after him, not to scare him but to let him know he did something wrong.

Troubleshooting the Turnaround

There are other common turnaround problems that might plague you. Here are some troubleshooting exercises to tackle them.

A horse that doesn't use his hindquarters correctly can spin on his outside hind leg or even swap ends, where his front legs trade places with his hind legs, otherwise known as bottle-spinning. Every time you feel that happening, drive the horse out of the spin and get after him a little bit. Don't let him become accustomed to spinning that way.

Then, bring him back to a tight little circle at the lope. Take your outside leg and push the horse's hip into the circle. Open the door to the inside by taking any pressure off your inside leg. If you have to, lay a spur on your horse to get the hip to the inside where the spin occurs. For example, if you want to spin to the left, lope off in a left lead, then take your right leg and press right behind the horse's right rib cage to push his hips to the left or inside. Open your left leg so nothing obstructs the horse from going to the inside.

Once he gets his hip up underneath himself, turn (or spin) him in that direction and lope out of it — about three quarters of the way out of the spin. Then lay your leg into him and turn him again. In this scenario, the horse spins, then lopes, then spins, then lopes. It really teaches him to hunt the spot to turn and squat with his hindquarters, making it easier for him to turn. In effect, his weight is shifted to his hindquarters and his inside hind leg, where the power to spin comes from.

You can try this exercise at a trot first if that helps you with your cuing and the horse with his cadence.

For a horse that drops his shoulder into the turn, one helpful exercise is to pick up the reins and hold his head between them, driving the horse into the bridle, asking him to give to pressure. That puts the horse in a collected frame and helps keep his shoulders up. He can't turn correctly if his shoulder drops, either inside or outside the spin.

Another problem is over-bending into the turnaround. The horse's body and neck should be straight in the spin, with just the chin slightly turned to the inside. All you should see is the corner of your horse's eye and a little of his chin. If you see more of his head and neck as you're turning, your horse's body is too bent to turn well and fast. His neck should be straight with his withers. To fix this, use your outside leg to push your horse's hip into the spin and use your outside rein to straighten the horse's neck. If need be, bring the neck back in line by dropping the outside rein down closer to your knee. That helps the horse's neck to align with his body.

TIPS

Time the Turnaround

Practice the turnaround fairly early in your training session. Don't lope the horse for a half hour and then expect him to be fresh enough to perform intricate maneuvers. If he gets tired, his attitude will suffer and your training session will fall apart.

A horse can also lead with his ear in a turnaround, which means he tilts his poll in the direction of the spin. Sometimes the inside shoulder drops into the spin, along with the tilted head. Lift the inside rein to bring the head back into line. Lower the lifted rein once the horse brings his head in line, but keep some tension on it to maintain the horse's head position.

From circles to speed control, lead changes to sliding stops and rollbacks to turnarounds, that's our complete maneuver regimen, built on solid fundamentals and the judicious use of pressure and release. Remember, as we said in the beginning of this book, the horse always knows where the pressure is not. His nature is to seek comfort and relief from pressure. It's a concept that makes sense to the horse, and it's at the heart of our entire reining training program.

The next stop? The horse show.

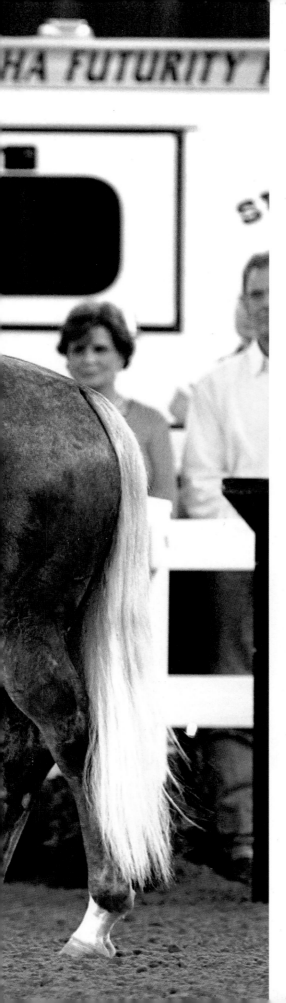

14

SHOW PREPARATION

After you've spent time learning to rein and having your horse trained to rein, it's time for both of you to be tested. The National Reining Horse Association has provided a level playing field, with its judging system, standard maneuvers and set of patterns.

In reining competition you show off how well broke your horse is and how well he guides. That's what reining is all about and the best way to do that is at a horse show, where conditions are the same for everyone and all riders and horses are judged equally against one another.

In this chapter, we'll talk about preparation, before and during a show.

It takes a ton of preparation, along with exceptional talent, to win any reining, much less an aged event such as a futurity or derby. Shown are Shawn and Wimpys Little Step, winners of the 2002 NRHA Futurity.

The Rule Book

Your first order of business is to read the NRHA Handbook (the official rule book) from cover to cover. Be thoroughly familiar with the rules and regulations, divisions, judge's scoring, patterns and penalties. It's your responsibility to know all about the sport in which you're competing, so don't rely on your friends or even your trainer to clue you in. It's also worthwhile to read the rule book at the beginning of every competition year, as the rules change, so stay on top of them.

It's really helpful for anyone new to the sport to volunteer as a judge's scribe or maybe even attend an NRHA judges course.

Good Exposure

Before you ever take your horse to a show, expose him to lots of different environments.

Haul your horse to as many different places as you can to accustom him to a variety of environments.

Otherwise, the first time you take him away from home, he'll be so anxious and disoriented that he won't show well for you. Horses like familiar things; they don't care for change. Some horses are just spookier than others, so you have to assess your horse's mentality as much as you do his talent.

At home, put up banners in your arena so your horse is used to things on the fence or wall, possibly flapping and even making noise. There are always sponsor banners at horse shows. Having lots of sponsors helps show management make enough money to put on the show. It's your job to accustom your horse to banners of all kinds and colors and in all sorts of places.

Haul your horse to many different arenas in your area — they could be your friends' facilities or the local fairgrounds. This kind of exposure gets him used to going into a trailer and coming out of it in strange places. Over time, he'll take one look at things as he steps out of your trailer and go, "ho-hum, just another arena." But this could take many trips down the road.

You can tell a lot about your horse's level of bravery just by being around him. If he jumps every time you walk by his stall or the dog runs by, you're probably looking at a lot of miles of seasoning ahead of you.

Get Ready, Get Set

Several days before the show, make a list of what you'll need to take with you — feed, buckets, blankets, first-aid kit. Consider loading some things into your horse trailer ahead of time so you won't have to throw them in at the last minute and risk leaving something important behind.

Clean your tack, saddle pads and protective boots. Take a spare bridle in case the one you normally wear breaks or you lose a Chicago screw.

Make sure your horse trailer is clean and in good shape. Perform any necessary maintenance. Check the brakes, lighting and tires, especially. It's a wise idea to have two spare tires just in case the worst happens. Of course, make sure you have tire-changing equipment.

If you have a living quarters trailer, outfit it a day or two before you leave. That way you're less likely to forget something.

If you don't have an LQ, reserve your motel room ahead of time so you're not hunting a place to stay after you drop off your horse at the show grounds.

Keep a file or a notebook with your membership card, your horse's competition license and his health papers. Have them all handy to put in your truck or trailer. Make extra copies

Make sure your tack and riding apparel are clean and in good repair before the show.

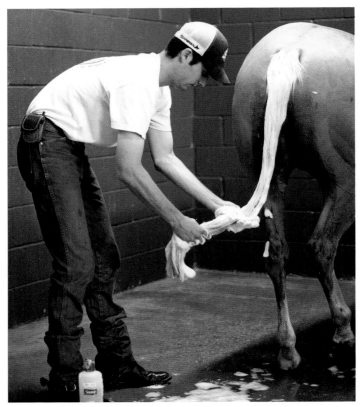

A meticulously clean horse is an absolute necessity for the show ring. Constant mane and tail care is all part of routine maintenance.

so you'll never be without them at a show. If you're missing any one of them, show management will likely not let you enter and your trip will be wasted. So make it a ritual to have your papers with you.

Grooming

Obviously, you must clip and bathe your horse before the show. However, there are grooming routines you should follow throughout the year, such as maintaining the mane and tail. They need constant work to remain long and beautiful, which is so necessary in today's show horse.

Braid your horse's tail and keep it in a tail bag or sock. Once a week, take it down, wash and condition it, along with his mane.

If you water your horse with buckets (instead of automatic waterers), make sure you tape the sides of the bucket so the tail braid or sack doesn't get caught in the bucket handle. It could pull out the whole tail.

Also, blunt cut any long tail hairs that drag the ground. When you back a horse during practice or in a show, you could inadvertently pull a huge chunk of tail hair out and it will take forever to grow back again.

Travel Schedule

For a regular weekend show, try to get there a day ahead of time. Drive there on a Thursday so you can settle in early and school your horse in the pen if you can. It's best to have at least two rides on the horse, either in the warm-up pen and show pen or as many as you can in the show pen.

Futurities are different. You'll need to be at the show grounds several days in advance to accustom your horse and yourself to the surroundings.

Show Day

Arrive at the show grounds early to feed and groom. Bathe your horse if he needs it and leave enough time for your horse to dry and digest his food before you ride. Getting there late will leave you rushed, and you'll tend to forget things under that kind of pressure.

If your horse appears a little too "bright-eyed and bushy-tailed," don't be embarrassed to longe him and work the freshness off. Wipe that smile right off his face and replace it with a workmanlike attitude. It's far better to do that than to chance him bucking or acting too playful in the warm-up pen.

Take the "fresh" of your horse in the warm-up pen. Keep your horse's tail braided or in a tail sack until it's time to show.

Backing up a horse anytime, but especially in the show pen, is a prime opportunity for the horse to step on and break off his tail hair. Prevent that by cutting it bluntly at the bottom, about level with his fetlocks.

Look for the posted draw so you can strategize for your run. If you drew first at 8:00 a.m., you should probably be at the show grounds by 5:00. If you're the fourth draw in the class, get on your horse at least an hour to an hour and a half before the class starts.

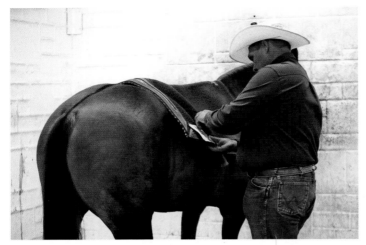

Put your number on your saddle pad when you first arrive at the show grounds, so you don't forget in the hustle and bustle of getting ready to show.

If you draw later in the class, determine how much time you'll need to warm up your horse, whether it's 10, 15 or 20 horses ahead of you. Some horses obviously take more time than others. You know your horse best; but if it's a new horse to you, you'd better plan on getting on him at least 20 horses ahead. We prefer a 20-horse margin even if we know we have enough time and our horses are ready.

Things happen and sometimes you can't help being late, but if you are in the habit of not allowing yourself enough time to prepare, you're setting yourself up to fail. If there are five or six horses before you go and your horse isn't clean or tacked up, his protective boots aren't on, and you don't have your hat, boots, spurs, chaps and number on, then you're asking for trouble.

Arena Strategy

The day before a show (or early the morning of if you didn't get there until the day of the show), look at the arena from the stands or, better yet, walk into it, either afoot or on a horse, to get a feel for where things are

Grooming before a class takes a lot of time, so get an early start. That way you're less likely to forget something important.

and how much space you have to perform your maneuvers. Don't let the first time you consider the inside of the pen be the second you enter the arena to show. Things happen so fast you won't know where you are in the pattern. As the saying goes, if you fail to plan, you plan to fail.

While looking at the arena, run the pattern through your mind, pick out specific stopping spots and see where the center is from the middle of the pen. Notice any banners on the arena walls and use them as your guide. For example, if there's a sponsor banner hanging at the area where you plan to stop, pick out a letter in the sponsor's name and plan your stop at that exact letter. Count the strides you'll have to come across the middle of the pen to change leads. This kind of preparation is almost like getting "in the zone" and, when you're there, it's a good feeling. You block everything out, and, all of a sudden, everything in the pen becomes perfectly clear. Watch a professional basketball or football player when they're in the zone. They can't miss the ball; their athletic responses are automatic. They can't do anything wrong. Being that prepared helps with any show-ring jitters as well.

Do this type of mental prep by yourself, not with a friend or your trainer. It takes only a couple of minutes, but it's vital to how you run your pattern.

If you're horseback during this prep, tear the pattern down by maneuvers and walk or lope quietly to the spots where maneuvers happen. See how much room you have to perform them.

Warm-Up Routine

Every show has a make-up pen, where you can school your horse at the last minute and await your turn before you enter the class. There's generally a paddock manager, who calls the numbers in their draw order. Be ready when your number is called; otherwise you might forfeit your turn.

Some shows have separate warm-up and make-up pens, but nonetheless, they're generally close to the competition arena. Have a set routine you go through as a warm-up drill: Check out all your navigation systems, make sure your horse is steering, stopping, circling, etc. Keep him quiet and relaxed. Don't pick any fights with him. You want him to be as willing as possible, not on the defensive.

Arrive at the make-up pen at least 20 horses before your draw.

Have a game plan and stick to it. Don't try something new on your horse right before you show. If you see another rider performing an interesting training technique, wait until you get home to try it out. You'll only confuse yourself and your horse if you introduce something new when you should be reinforcing the familiar.

Warm up the horse sufficiently, but don't show him sweaty. Factor in enough time to allow him to cool down and dry off. You want to present a fresh picture to the judge.

Also, don't ride your horse so much that he runs out of air before you show. A lot of runs are wasted in the warm-up pen. You want your horse physically capable of putting in a solid run and he can't do that when he's tired. You might even have your trainer, spouse or friend watch your warm-up. They can see little things that you might be doing wrong or even tell you when your horse has had

Be ready when the paddock manager calls your number.

enough and you need to back off. Sometimes adrenaline can get the best of you and you forget when to quit.

Another important thing to remember in the warm-up pen is etiquette. There are understood rules about how to school your horse. For example, riders circling their horses have the right-of-way over those working on other maneuvers. Typically, riders work on whatever maneuvers they feel are important at the time, but sometimes there's a period designated for only fencing or stopping — one side of the arena, then the other. They take turns or are at least careful not to interfere with another rider's rundown. Be cognizant of your fellow riders and what they're doing at all times. You can easily cause an accident if your horse runs into another horse. Surviving the warm-up pen is one of the rites of passage for all rookie reiners and is a given for experienced non-pros and open riders. Keep your head up and eyes open.

Show Time!

Just prior to going into the pen, maybe one horse before your turn, visualize your pattern again. Think what your approach for the first set of maneuvers will be. That will get you

This is what you've worked and waited for. Enjoy yourself!

started off in the right frame of mind. Also, you can draw the pattern in the air with your index finger. This is something you'll see a lot of top reining pros doing, so don't let it bother you to do so. Do whatever it takes to help you remember your pattern and perform it with precision. That's the name of the game and the way to higher scores.

Also, now is the time to get over the fact that "everyone is watching me." If you're showing your horse, you're on display. It's all part of the game and you're a designated player. Showing horses can be one of the most humbling experiences of your life.

During your run, you might mess up on a maneuver. It happens to all of us. Try not to let it rattle you and your concentration. Go on to the next maneuver as if nothing happened. The main thing is to not quit trying. There isn't anything you'll ever do in a reining pattern that most pros haven't done many times over, so learn from your mistakes and go on.

For every time you show your horse, you'll probably need to go to three schooling shows to get his mind right again. Horses get very pen- and pattern-wise. It doesn't take them any time at all to figure out what happens next. Your horse might anticipate a maneuver or try to out-fox you in some way during a run. You'll need to school him under show conditions to get him listening to you again. This is true for any age horse, from a 3-year-old to an aged horse.

Somewhere in every pattern, you'll find something come apart, something that needs a little work. It could be a lead change, a roll-back or a rundown to a stop. Schooling shows help where practice can't. They offer actual live competition conditions, something you can't re-create at home.

Have Fun

The main reason to show your horse is to have fun. It's that way for us, as well. Even though we make our living at it and that might put it into another ballpark, so to speak, it must be enjoyable. Being too intense takes all the fun out of it.

Showing horses is a social event. You get to travel to different places, catch up with old friends, meet new ones and see a lot of great horses perform. What could be better?

So, go to the show and have fun. If you bomb out, say you go off pattern or your horse gets a little too close to the judge, laugh about it and go on. Don't dwell on it and punish yourself. There's always another reining.

15

PATTERN STRATEGY

Putting maneuvers together in a smooth, precise and correct pattern is the ultimate goal in reining. When you walk into the arena to show what you've got to the judge, all your time, training and efforts are on the line. This is what you've worked so hard for. But things happen so fast that you don't have time to think about anything except your next maneuver. This is when all your preparation comes into play, and you execute your game plan. And, believe us, you need a game plan.

There's an old saying that goes, "If you fail to plan, you plan to fail." We never enter any show, anywhere, without planning a strategy for success. Even if we've been to the same show grounds many times and have run the patterns

Planning a strategy for each run helps ensure a smooth, precise execution. Shown are Craig and Commanders Nic, winners of the 2004 NRHA Derby.

TRAINER'S TIP

The Slow Walk

Train your horse to walk slowly but purposefully in your practice at home. Teach him to take one step at a time by squeezing with both legs as he's standing still. When he takes one step forward, release the pressure and the horse should stop. Allow him to stay there and rest. He should wait until you ask him to move. Squeeze again and ask for another step. When he moves his leg forward, release. He should move slowly one step at a time, almost like an arena trail horse.

The advantage of this is that you have complete control over the horse's body and leg movement. This is helpful in such things as lead departures that happen in the middle of the pen on a walk-in pattern. You can set his body up by side-passing one step at a time. Lay one leg against his rib cage and ask him to move off it to the side. For example, to side-pass to the left, apply right leg pressure at the horse's girth or just behind it. When the horse moves his body one step to the left, release your right leg. Repeat with one step at a time until it becomes an automatic response on the horse's part. Then hold the pressure steady. The horse will learn to keep side-passing until he feels the release of pressure.

hundreds of times, we still strategize our every move before we enter the show pen.

In this chapter, we'll tear down the parts of a standard NRHA pattern and give you tips and some training techniques on how to handle the maneuvers, plus troubleshoot any common problem areas.

It all begins with your entry into the pen. According to the official NRHA patterns, there are walk-in and run-in patterns, and how you approach either sets the tone for your entire run.

Walk-in Pattern

The correct way to enter a walk-in pattern is slowly, with your horse relaxed and holding his head level or slightly down. Don't walk down the middle of the arena. According to the rule book, you're supposed to walk 20 feet from the wall or fence.

If your horse tends to be spooky or you can tell he's on edge, don't walk him right next to the wall. The crowd is too close and could

For a walk-in pattern, position yourself at least 20 feet from the wall or fence.

make enough noise or movement to spook the horse unnecessarily. Walk the horse farther out from the wall, but not so far it could be considered the middle of the pen.

However, there are times when you might want to get a bit closer to the wall. Fast-walking horses give the impression that they're in a hurry. If your horse has a quick pace, position him a bit closer to the wall so it doesn't look like he's walking as fast. Also, it takes more time to get to the center that way, so it creates more of an illusion of a slow walk to the judge. Some horses just walk faster than others, but you want to present the best picture you can to the judge in everything you do, and your walk to the center is the first opportunity the judge has to evaluate you and your horse.

The opposite of too fast is too slow. It's possible to walk so slowly that you irritate the judge because you're delaying the reining. Strike a happy medium between pokey slow and chargey fast.

When he comes to the center, ask your horse to stop, and then put your hand down, which is a signal to relax. Your horse should come to a complete standstill, put his head down and relax before you ever ask him for a maneuver. This shows that your horse is calm and paying attention to you. You want him to learn that the center is a resting place.

After your horse stops in the center, look at the judge. Acknowledge him in this way, which tells him that you're ready to work. If you're at all nervous, take a deep breath and count to five slowly. One Mississippi, two Mississippi, three Mississippi, four Mississippi, five Mississippi. You're now ready to begin your pattern, which usually starts with either circles or spins.

Run-in Pattern

A run-in pattern is a more challenging beginning to your run. (All of them require speed followed by a sliding stop.) It's best for non-pros to simply lope in, rather than run in at a dead gallop. You don't want to unnecessarily ruffle your horse and cause him to become excited right off the bat.

In the warm-up pen, before you ask for the lope, make sure your horse is in the bridle and listening to you. Jiggle the reins back and forth and ask your horse to give you his head. You don't want to have to worry about steering issues as you're loping, so take care of that business before you enter the gate.

TRAINER'S TIP

Head Down

Teach your horse to drop his head on command by applying gentle but steady pressure with both of your legs on the horse's sides to keep the horse from moving backward. Take a rein in each hand and jiggle (slightly pull) them in a back and forth motion. When the horse gives his jaw one way in response to your rein pressure, release. Then jiggle the other rein to ask the horse to give his jaw to the other side. Release as soon as he gives it. When the horse drops his head in the position you're looking for, release both reins and let the horse rest.

Once the horse's head is down, the horse might pick it up and look out across the arena. Return to putting pressure on his rib cage with your legs and jiggle the reins once more.

You can keep bumping the reins until the horse almost puts his chin on the ground. That's extreme, and you don't have to go that far, but it's a good exercise to do. You don't have to be harsh on a horse, just aggravate him enough to where he puts his head or body where you want it.

Teaching a horse to put his head down on command helps keep his attention on you in the show ring.

Some arenas don't have the entry gate in the center, so you'll have to walk your horse slowly to the center of the wall or fence and begin your run from there. Start out slowly and build your speed in the rundown. Hunt for the spot where you're going to stop.

Every horse seems to stop best on a favorite lead. It might be the right or left one, but know your horse's best stopping lead and choose that one for your entry rundown. You're looking to make your first impression to the judge a good one, so plan your strategy for the run-in well in advance.

Another reason to take it easy while running through the gate is for the sake of your horse's longevity. Blasting through a gate can

In a run-in pattern, pick the spot you want to stop ahead of time.

make some horses lose it mentally, and the rest of the run will be ruined with a flighty and uncontrollable horse. Pros often save their blast-in runs for the big money. At a regular weekend show or smaller futurity, they run their horses judiciously and save the big-guns-a-blazing entries for the bigger paydays.

If you know your pattern the week or even the night before a show, practice your run-in ahead of time.

If you have the type of horse that's exceptionally nervous about getting into the arena, you might have to walk him in through the gate, then start your run slowly and build to your stop.

It's not a bad idea to rehearse it both ways and see what's best for your horse.

Circles and Lead Departures

Many walk-in patterns begin with circles started in the center of the pen. Circles are the hardest maneuver to plus (score a plus ½ to 1 ½) in a reining. A lot of unfortunate things can happen. Your horse can take the

Before departing into a circle, ask your horse to flex at the poll. This gets his mind on you and helps him collect to take the proper lead.

wrong lead, fall out of lead, switch leads or run off out of control. Many of these penalties happen when the horse runs at top speed.

NRHA patterns call for large fast circles, but that doesn't mean out of control. If you're not comfortable with running your horse at blazing speed, don't. Just gallop enough to mark a 0. You must know what speed your horse can handle mentally and physically. If your horse can manage a high speed and still come back to you, then fine. By all means, show off what your horse can do. But if you think he'll fall out of lead going fast or take

BUILD SPEED IN CIRCLES

1. In this right lead departure, the horse flexes at the poll and gives to the bit, thus preparing himself for the lope.

2. Collected, the horse drives with his hindquarters, lifting his back as he moves into the lope.

3. The rider builds speed slowly; he doesn't burst into a gallop from a standstill.

4. When the rider asks for more speed, the horse stretches his stride in the large, fast circle.

5. The horse is wide open, but still remains in a collected frame. Note the horse's consistent head position throughout the lead departure, slow lope and gallop.

the bit and run, then go only as fast as the two of you can handle and get the pattern right.

Since all circles begin in the center of the pen with their lead departures and lead changes, it's important to make that a place where nothing too abrupt or scary happens to the horse. If he starts anticipating things or thinks the center is where he gets jabbed with a spur, you'll soon have an anxious animal on your hands and your pattern and score will suffer for it.

Before you begin a circle, ask your horse to give to the bit and, in so doing, you get his attention. That one little cue — to give in the face (bend at the poll) — helps get your horse's mind on you, so your horse can prepare to lope.

Walk a few steps before you cue your horse to depart into a lope. Some riders prefer to start from a standstill, but things are less hurried and abrupt if you ask for the lead departure from a walk.

Lope off slowly at first, even if it's a large fast circle you have to perform. You don't want to blow your horse's mind right away by kicking him into high gear from the get-go.

After a few strides, build your speed. There are several ways to drive your horse into a faster speed. One is to push your rein hand forward on his neck and use your legs, either by squeezing or bumping his rib cage. Another signal to increase speed is kissing or clucking. Use whatever cue you've trained your horse with.

Leaning forward in the saddle also gives your horse the go-forward-fast cue and is used by most pros to ask for speed. When you get up over your horse's withers, it's like riding a race horse, and most horses respond by quickening their strides and moving from a lope into a gallop.

Don't look down at your horse while circling. Instead, look ahead at where you want to go.

When you return to the center for a small, slow circle, sit back in the saddle and put your rein hand back down in front of the saddle horn. This encourages your horse to move into the slower lope. Quiet your whole body and your horse will take this as a cue to slow down.

Some horses you have to kick every stride just to work up a gallop. Others you have to sit extremely quietly so they don't inadvertently take more cues from you to go faster. They're going plenty fast as it is.

Transitions Between Circles

Some patterns call for large fast and small slow circles and lead changes between them

For large, fast circles, lean forward in the saddle and "chase" the horse with the reins.

at various speeds. The transitions between the circles are the key to scoring well.

For example, Pattern #9 calls for a left-lead departure from the center into a small slow circle, followed by two large fast circles. Don't slow down four strides before you get to the center and then change leads to the right. Wait until you get to the center, change leads, then slow down and go into the next set of circles to the right, which begin with a small slow, followed by two large fast.

In the small slow circle, ask for the lead departure, then drop your rein hand and sit quietly with slack in the reins. A little light rein contract is okay, but don't have a tight rein in a slow circle. It shows the judge that your horse is chargey and not listening to you.

As you ride your circles, look for the center of the arena before you get there and ride up the center of the circle in a straight line.

After completing the small slow circle in the center, transition to the large fast circle by leaning your body forward in the saddle and pushing your rein hand forward. Keep your arm straight out in front of you as if you were pointing toward your horse's ears.

Pattern #10 calls for two large fast circles to the right, followed by a small slow, then a change to a left-lead small slow circle, followed by two large fast circles. In this instance, you'd depart into the right lead from the center, then build your speed, but slowly, for a couple of strides. Remember to lean forward, push your hand forward and cluck or kiss to your horse, whatever cue you use to ask him for speed. You should be at your top speed when you round the top of the right circle.

After your second large fast circle, sit down in the center and bring your rein hand down to just above the saddle horn to slow your horse. Change leads to the left in the center on a straight line. The first circle is slow, followed by two large fast.

Lead Changes

When you come across the middle for a lead change, strive to change in the exact center. That shows the judge a lot of precision on your part.

But before you get to the center to change, which would be approximately at the top of the circle, straighten the line of the circle. In other words, instead of riding a completely round circle, make a D-shaped circle and execute your changes down the straight line of the D. There are around a half dozen strides

down the center line of most circles where you can lope straight. That gives you enough time and distance to nail your lead change in the actual center of the pen by asking for it around the third stride. After you change, continue loping straight for a few strides before you hit the top of the next circle.

In small arenas you might not have a half dozen strides down the middle to play with, but, no matter what, try to shape your circles into a D and perform your lead changes on straightaways. This helps keep your horse from ducking, diving and dropping his shoulder into his changes, a habit that will only get worse over time.

Use subtle leg cues to change from one lead to the other. However, if your horse is broke to change leads by an obvious neck-rein cue, that's fine, but the less rein-hand movement, the better, as far as how it looks to a judge.

The most important thing is to keep your horse quiet and soft through the lead changes. They should look effortless, and as if your horse read your mind.

As you come down the middle of the circle, straighten the line your horse is on before the lead change.

As you come down the center to change, you might feel your horse leaning or dropping a shoulder into the circle. This will definitely affect the quality of your lead change. Keep your outside leg on him to keep him straight. For example, if you are circling left and coming to the center to change to the right, but your horse is leaning hard to the left, dropping his left shoulder into the left circle, keep your left leg on him to close that doorway. That should help straighten him, so you can change to the right lead.

Turnarounds

The center of the pen can cause anxiety for both horse and rider, but you both have to be relaxed there in order to do your best, whether it's a lead departure or turnaround.

To perform a turnaround, make sure your horse is standing squarely with the judge, not cocked at an angle. Start straight and complete the required number of turns the pattern calls for.

For example, in turning to the left, when you lay your right bridle rein on the horse's neck, he should look left and begin his turn. There shouldn't be a pause or hesitation on

For turnarounds, pick a spot to begin your count before you start spinning.

your horse's part. If you have to repeatedly pick up your rein hand and lay the rein on your horse's neck to ask him to turn and your horse ignores your request, you'll lose points. If your horse doesn't respond immediately, use leg pressure discreetly to reinforce your rein cue. Try not to let the judge see you bump him with your outside leg, just squeeze your leg or press your spur slowly to get a response.

Start slowly and increase your speed as you turn.

Pick a spot, either the judge or maybe an arena banner, to look at as you count your spins. If you don't pick a spot ahead of time, you take the chance of over- or under-spinning. You can lose a lot of points that way, so work to stay as straight as you can with the starting point.

It doesn't work well or look good to pick a spot, then continually jerk your head back to it as your horse turns around. Keep your head and your focus straight. You'll look more professional and have a better chance of seeing your counting spot.

Also, don't focus on the ground, as that will make you dizzy.

If it works for you, count out loud during your practice in the pen before the show. After the first revolution, say "One" as that spot comes into your view. Continue with "Two," "Three" and "Four." Then, when it comes time to compete, you can count silently. But no matter what, it's okay to count out loud if you feel it helps you to keep on pattern.

However, one big drawback to counting out loud is that your horse will hear you and possibly anticipate that you're asking him to stop. He might stop his momentum during the spin and then you'll lose points.

Between spins, pause or hesitate for around five seconds. Give yourself and your horse a chance to get your bearings. Allow your horse to relax before you ask for the second set of spins. If you don't, you'll only teach him to be anxious in the middle of the pen, something he might never get over. It might not happen the first or second time you ram and jam him in the middle, but it will happen. So slow down and take your time in the center of the pen, whether it's between spins or for lead departures.

Rein-fix

Sometimes your reins shift during the turnaround, even flop over on the other side of the horse's neck. Split reins, the traditional reins used in reining, should be held in your left hand and hang on the left side of the horse's neck.

Fix them between spins and put them back where they hang straight again. To do that correctly, remember not to grab hold of the reins in front of your left hand or to change rein hands as you straighten them out. That would result in a 0 score because you've then put both hands on the reins and the rules say you must ride one-handed.

The proper way to fix your rein tails is to use your right hand to pull the reins behind your left hand and over to the left side of the neck.

4 ¼ spins

There are some patterns (such as #1 and #7) where you have to run in, stop, and back to the center before you start your turnarounds. When you back, stop square with the judge. Then spin four times to the right. Pick a point on the far wall to be your "spot" and start your count after the first revolution. Hesitate; don't immediately go into your second set of spins. Allow your horse to regroup.

The second set of spins is to the left, but you make four and one quarter revolutions, which makes it easy to get out of sync in your counting. The trick is to look over your left shoulder at the judge and use him as your starting point. That way you don't really count the first quarter turn. Start your count "One" as you see the judge for the second time and continue on through four spins. When you do it that way, your four and one quarter spins will take care of themselves, and you'll never over- or under-turn.

The Shut Off

When you ask your horse to shut down the turnaround, say "whoa" quietly and put your hand down, but don't touch his neck. That's your horse's cue to stop and not move. Don't have your rein hand up in the air because there's a good possibility that your horse will over-spin, run into the high reins, tilt his head and neck and the whole thing will look ugly.

Rundown and Stop

The secret to most good stops is the rundown. On the approach or rundown to a stop, your horse should "go through the gears" in his buildup of speed — from first, second, third to fourth gear, etc. It's not good to go from first gear to fifth gear. Build speed in increments, don't go slowly, then blast to a stop.

Depending on the pattern you're performing, rundowns to a stop occur either on the straightaway going down the middle or in a horseshoe shape around the ends of the arena.

In either case, don't miss your markers or cones by not stopping in the pattern's designated area. If you miss a marker, it's a 2-point penalty and there's no way to make up those two points, no matter how good a stop your horse has.

For a horseshoe rundown (around the sides and end of the arena) begin on the correct lead, which, in all cases, is the leading leg to the inside of the arena. In other words, if you're loping to the left, be on the left lead in your rundown or vice-versa.

On the last part of the horseshoe or rundown, make sure your horse's shoulders are square, not leaning one way or the other. He won't be able to stop well if he's dropping either shoulder.

For a good stop, the horse's shoulders should be square, not leaning one way or the other.

Increase your speed incrementally and build to a smooth stop, within the designated markers (second and third cones). A good place to start building your speed is after you pass the first cone or marker.

Kiss or cluck or use your go-faster cue to build your speed. Make sure your horse accelerates to a stop. That's the only way a good stop can happen. If your horse is crooked, drops a shoulder, sets up too early or slows down at all in the final rundown, your stop will suffer. The latter, going from fifth gear to fourth gear, will mess up a stop faster than anything in the world.

To stop, say the proverbial "whoa." If your horse was trained properly, that's all he should need to put on the brakes; but, of course, there are times when you'll have to

Shove your feet forward in the saddle and use your legs as shock absorbers during sliding stops.

pull on the reins. That doesn't look nearly as pretty as a loose-rein stop, so strive to achieve that winning stop.

Rider's Stopping Position

During rundowns you need to be in a different seat position than you are in the circles. Your center of gravity should be farther back in the saddle. If you lean forward during a hard, sliding stop, your inertia might catapult you toward the horse's neck — not a pretty sight to the judge. Once you turn the corner on a horseshoe rundown, sit back and drive with your hips and legs to the stop.

To ensure a secure seat in the saddle, push your legs forward in the stirrups and scoot your seat bones under you and back toward the cantle. In effect, you're leaning back. If you were to drop a plumb line down through your shoulders, it would fall behind your hips; that's how far back you should lean. And the faster you run toward the stop, the more you sit back in the saddle.

Also, pay attention to the rest of your body. Your head should be up, not looking down. Your shoulders should be square, not leaning or twisting one way or the other. Your horse feels every single movement you make and if your body is crooked in the saddle, it might make him stop crooked, just to compensate for your weight shift.

When you say "whoa," shove your feet forward and your tailbone back into the saddle. That's also a cue to stop for horses trained that way, which ours are. To maintain your seat in a hard stop, you'll have to position yourself this way. Your back and your feet take the shock out of the stop.

If you sit up straight or lean forward in your rundown, then try to sit back one stride before the stop, it'll be difficult to get in sync with your horse. He could easily scotch or prop to a stop and throw you forward.

The "whoa" cue releases everything. When you say the magic word and shove your feet forward, release all rein pressure. Allow your horse to melt to a stop. But don't put your reins down on the horse's neck until he gets his hind legs back up under him again. Only then is the stop complete.

Some riders apply rein pressure while they say "whoa;" and that's okay too, but don't raise your hand prior to saying "whoa." That only confuses your horse and he might blow right through the bit. He won't know when the real stop should begin, and the whole picture for the judge won't be good.

Rollback

Other than the final stop, you'll have to roll back out of your stops and continue the pattern. On a good rollback, your horse should come 180 degrees over his hip and run back in the same tracks he made in the rundown.

To roll back after a particularly deep stop, when your horse's hind feet might be up toward your feet, allow your horse to raise himself before you ask him to roll back over his hocks. Give him a chance to get his hocks under him again, so he can physically perform the rollback.

One good rollback exercise to school your horse with is to turn him to the inside once in awhile, rather than always to the outside, which is the correct way in a reining. This keeps your horse guessing and helps prevent him from hurrying to the stop, leaning in toward the wall.

Another thing you can do in practice to prevent anticipation: After a right rollback, most horses know that they have to go to the right around the arena. Change that by going to the left instead. This also helps keep a horse from charging out of the rollback.

Your inspiration was our motivation in writing this book. We hope that after reading it you appreciate reining and the reining horse even more than you did before. Reining is truly one of the fastest growing equine sports in the world, mainly because of the incredible athlete that's your partner and the fact that he encourages you to excel in your own horsemanship.

Throughout, we've offered our time-tested training techniques and strategies for success. Our goal was to try to help you select the right horse, maintain him in peak condition, lay the foundation for training, train with understanding, perfect the reining maneuvers and compete with a game plan. The road map is laid out for you. The journey is now yours. Good luck and good reining!

PROFILE:
SHAWN FLARIDA

Few youngsters know exactly what they want to be when they grow up. And fewer yet ever become their dream. Shawn Flarida did. From his earliest remembrances, he knew he wanted to be a horse trainer — no doubt in his mind. From the third grade on, his goal was to train and show horses. He does both at the top of his game and today the 38-year-old trainer is one of only two NRHA Two Million Dollar Riders.

Growing up in Wapakoneta, Ohio, in a house full of four boys, Shawn became involved with horses at a young age. They were a hobby for his father, Bill, who'd wanted to be a horse trainer as a young man, but Shawn's grandparents didn't think Bill could make a living at it. They never could have dreamed that their grandson would become one of the most successful horse trainers in the country.

Shawn was heavily influenced by his father, who, according to Shawn, is a great horseman, his mentor and best friend. Throughout grade school and high school, Shawn was fortunate enough to have his dad in his corner for local horse shows. They'd also sit in the stands at major horse events, such as the NRHA Futurity and All American Quarter Horse Congress, and evaluate what they saw in the arena. Then they'd go home and try out the techniques they saw the big trainers perform.

Shawn and his dad also attended jackpot reinings in Findlay, Ohio, put on by Dale Wilkinson, acknowledged today as the "Father of Reining" and inducted into the NRHA Hall of Fame. Wilkinson would offer Shawn advice and critique his performance, giving the young Flarida some things to work on before the next jackpot. Shawn's introduction to the sport was as good as it gets from the start. Still today, Shawn's father rides with him once a week and coaches him from the sidelines at horse shows.

When he was about 12 years old, Shawn met Craig Schmersal, who rode horses with Shawn's older brother, Mike, a two-time NRHA Futurity winner. The two have been good friends ever since. Like Shawn, Craig is an NRHA Million Dollar Rider, and the two have collaborated on a set of instructional tapes ("Good as Gold Reining") as well as this book.

Shawn started showing Quarter Horses at age 8, but began his reining career in earnest in high school, when he competed and placed sixth in the 1988 NRHA Non Pro Futurity on Kings Sara San. Right out of school, he went pro at age 19. He charged only $350 a month and had to take in a few western pleasure horses to pay the bills. But he always preferred reining, and it didn't take long for him to specialize in the sport. He's had a barn full of good horses ever since.

With the help of owners and breeders, such as Carol Harris, Sammy Ely, John Essman, Bob Stinner and Mark Schols, Shawn rocketed to the forefront of the pro ranks with horses who've made NRHA history — the likes of Itsa Bingo Greyhound, Zan Freckles Hickory and Mr Kali Jac. When he was 21, Shawn entered and made the NRHA Futurity finals on three horses, not an easy task for even the most seasoned of pros.

Shawn has continued his upward march in all categories of NRHA competition, winning both world championships and major aged events. He's a three-time NRHA Futurity champion. His first triumph came on Wimpys Little Step in 2002, when the pair marked the highest score in NRHA Futurity history — 233. He followed that victory with another in 2004 on Smart Spook and in 2005 on KL Lil Conquistador.

When the NRHA branched out to include United States Equestrian Team (now United States Equestrian Federation) reining competition, Shawn made sure he was part of the scene, knowing how important riding at an international level is to the western sport. He qualified three horses for the first USET Festival of Champions in Gladstone, N. J., in 1999, and returned with mounts for the 2000 and 2001 events. In 2001, he was a member of the USA Nation's Cup gold medal team and won an individual silver medal on San Jo Freckles.

The latter earned him a berth to represent the United States at the 2002 World Equestrian Games in Jerez, Spain. There he was the individual gold medalist on San Jo Freckles, and Team USA was the team gold medal winner (Craig was a member of Team USA).

Shawn continues to compete at the international level abroad and in the United States, garnering more accolades, such as champion of the 2006 FEI World Reining Masters.

Shawn married his high school sweetheart, Michele, after a six-year courtship. They have three children, Cody, Courtney and Sam, and have established their home and reining horse training center in Springfield, Ohio.

The Flaridas: top – Michele, Cody, Shawn, bottom – Courtney, and Sam.

PROFILE: CRAIG SCHMERSAL

Craig Schmersal has always had a passion for horses, so much so that he turned it into his life's work. And it shows! He's one of the NRHA's leading money-earners, but even more importantly, he has a reputation for training and showing champion horses that last. The reason they do — Craig's approach and techniques produce a willing, trainable athlete that enjoys his job every day he does it.

Like his co-author, Craig has wanted to become a horse trainer since childhood, and like Shawn, Craig has his father to thank for his solid beginning in the horse industry. To top it all off, he, too, is in his mid-30s (35 in 2007) and a member of the elite NRHA Million Dollar Rider club, as well.

Raised in Columbus Grove, Ohio, Craig started riding when he was 8 years old after a trip to the All American Quarter Horse Congress encouraged his equestrian career.

However, his first horses were Appaloosas, including some pleasure horses he constantly tried to turn into reiners.

Craig has been riding horses for the public since he was a freshman in high school, sometimes with as many as eight a day to ride. His dad, Chuck Schmersal, supported his son's passion every way he could. Chuck would make sure his son got to a local indoor arena to ride his horses every night after school, and he arranged for Craig to spend summers with other top reiners, such as two-time NRHA Futurity winner Mike Flarida (Shawn's brother). Craig met and made friends with Shawn at that time. Besides this book, they've partnered on a series of instructional videos titled "Good as Gold Reining."

Also as a youngster, Craig rode at top reining barns on Long Island, New York. People such as Henry and Elaine Uvino and Joe Annunziata gave him good horses to show and he didn't let them down.

Craig began his NRHA career as a teenager and quickly scaled the heights to the NRHA Top Ten Youth standings. His first success was on Leo Money Step, on whom he won two 14-18 Youth classes at the 1988 Joe Cody Classic.

Craig turned pro as soon as he could and has never looked back since. Between the NRHA's major aged events and the association's year-end standings, Craig has always been on the sport's A-list of trainers and competitors. He started his climb to the top placing in the top five of the 1991 and 1992 NRHA Limited Open Futurities, then earned two NRHA world titles on the great Cee Blair Sailor, owned by David Connor. Craig and the spectacular stallion, who eventually was named to the NRHA Hall of Fame, earned 90 paychecks out of 92 classes, including a prestigious win at the Americana in Augsberg, Germany.

Craig's notoriety was growing and in the mid-1990s he went to work with trainer Randy Paul in Scottsdale, Arizona, where he met and married his wife, Ginger. A Top 10 NRHA non-pro, Ginger has been instrumental to Craig as a business manager and a set of knowledgeable "eyes" to critique his training and show-ring efforts.

The couple, along with their two boys, Chris and Nick, moved to Temecula, California, in 1998, where they started Schmersal Reining Horses. Craig also enters National Reined Cow Horse Association competitions, and has been a finalist in the NRCHA Snaffle Bit Futurity and a champion of the NRHA Derby.

Craig has been in the finals of the NRHA Futurity every year for the last decade and has become an international reining star as well. Riding Tidal Wave Jack, he was part of the gold medal Team USA at the 2002 World Equestrian Games in Jerez, Spain, and won the FEI World Reining Masters in Manerbio, Italy.

Three Quarter Horse stallions Craig has trained and campaigned and in which he owns a partnership — Tidal Wave Jack, Commanders Nic and Mister Montana Nic — are testament to the longevity of his training program. All are NRHA Futurity finalists that went on to become earners of more than $100,000. Commanders Nic is the current NRHA all-time money-earning horse with more than $250,000 in earnings. Two other NRHA finalist stallions the Schmersals own and stand are Wrangle Whiz, also the earner of over $100,000 and Gunslider, who's registered with both the AQHA and APHA and is an NRBC Derby finalist, as well.

In 2006, Craig continued his winning ways by capturing the American Quarter Horse Association senior reining championship onboard Mr Dual Rey and by placing fourth in the NRHA Futurity on Sparkling Waves, by Tidal Wave Jack.

From the East Coast to the West Coast and anywhere in between, Craig has been a success every step of the way, no matter where he puts on his hat and spurs. In 2005, he and Ginger purchased Hickory Creek Ranch in Overbrook, Oklahoma, where they built their home and training facility.

The Schmersals: standing Ginger and Craig, kneeling Nick and Chris.

PROFILE:
KATHY SWAN

Kathy Swan considers herself one of the lucky ones to be able to make a living out of what she loves to do – reading, writing and riding horses.

A lifelong horsewoman, Kathy has explored many trails. She's earned local, regional and national awards in both American Quarter Horse and American Paint Horse Association competition, in a variety of English and western classes. She's also won in North American Trail Ride Conference competition and in hunter trials. Breeding Quarter Horses and Paints had been a serious hobby of her for years, but she's also owned Arabians, Thoroughbreds and Andalusians. Today, she's an avid trail rider and enjoys exploring the West horseback on the family's two ex-reining horses.

Kathy has won awards for both her writing and her photography. She has a broad background in the equine publication industry: news editor at the *Quarter Horse News*, editor of *Horseman* and *Horse & Rider*, and associate editor at *Western Horseman*. Currently, she's the editor of the *Western Horseman* book division.

Other Western Horseman titles by the writer include *Ride Smart by Craig Cameron*, and *Natural Horse-Man-Ship* and *Raise Your Hand if You Love Horses* by Pat Parelli. Published under the EquiMedia banner she wrote *Reining: the Art of Performance in Horses* by Bob Loomis.

Kathy lives in Scottsdale, Arizona, with her husband Rick and their well-loved horses, cats and dog.